Gebirgsjäger

Gebirgsjäger

German Mountain Troops, 1935–1945

Jean-Denis Lepage

Pen & Sword
MILITARY

First published in Great Britain in 2023 by
Pen & Sword Military
An imprint of
Pen & Sword Books Ltd
Yorkshire – Philadelphia

ISBN 978 1 39904 478 3

A CIP catalogue record for this book is
available from the British Library.

Typeset by Mac Style
Printed in the UK by CPI Group (UK) Ltd, Croydon, CR0 4YY.

Pen & Sword Books Limited incorporates the imprints of Atlas, Archaeology,
Aviation, Discovery, Family History, Fiction, History, Maritime, Military,
Military Classics, Politics, Select, Transport, True Crime, Air World,
Frontline Publishing, Leo Cooper, Remember When, Seaforth Publishing,
The Praetorian Press, Wharncliffe Local History, Wharncliffe Transport,
Wharncliffe True Crime and White Owl.

For a complete list of Pen & Sword titles please contact

PEN & SWORD BOOKS LIMITED
47 Church Street, Barnsley, South Yorkshire, S70 2AS, England
E-mail: enquiries@pen-and-sword.co.uk
Website: www.pen-and-sword.co.uk

Or

PEN AND SWORD BOOKS
1950 Lawrence Rd, Havertown, PA 19083, USA
E-mail: Uspen-and-sword@casematepublishers.com
Website: www.penandswordbooks.com

CONTENTS

INTRODUCTION

The origins of modern Alpine troops could be traced back to comparatively recent times, although a number of commanders (some of the greatest there have ever been) managed to lead their armies in mountainous regions. For example Hannibal the famous Carthagian general crossed the Alps in 218 BC during the Second Punic War before invading Italy. In 1800 the French Emperor Napoleon made a difficult and daring crossing of the St Bernard Pass in the Alps allowing his army to surprise the Austrians in Italy by winning the Battle of Marengo – a feat immortalized on canvas by the artist Jacques-Louis David.

Whoever tried to challenge the hostile mountainous environment could also come under attack from small gangs of local natives who could hold up a force much larger than their own for a considerable time. These rebels knew the mountainous areas well, and were often adept at conducting small-scale guerilla actions against conventional forces. A celebrated and anonymous medieval epic poem (entitled the *Song of Roland* written in the eleventh century) tells the tale of the Frankish Emperor Charlemagne whose rearguard commanded by Count-Paladin Roland was ambushed in 778 by Basque tribesmen at the Roncevaux Pass in the Pyrenees Mountains.

Such was military thinking in the past, that mountainous regions were not considered suitable terrain for warfare. Commanders in the few examples above, would on most occasions bypass mountainous areas. It was actually quite recently – in the late nineteenth century – that three European countries pioneered the use of specialized mountain troops: Italy with their Alpini Corps, France with the Chasseurs Alpins troops, and the Austro-Hungarian Empire with Gebirgsjäger. Until the First World War Germany had no real mountain troops as the defence of Germany's southern mountain regions fell to the Austro-Hungarian Army.

Obviously mountain troops were made up from men who were local to the mountains of their country, men who had a sound knowledge of mountainous terrain and were able to conduct both offensive and defensive action in this environment. Civilian mountainers and local hunters could also be employed as guides for the main body of the army who would have to pass over hostile and mountainous regions. When properly militarized they could be used as spearhead units at the forefront of an assault. There was however a distinct lack of men with alpine knowledge in Germany. Therefore mountaineering organizations and alpine clubs were set up with the aims of teaching the finer points of mountaineering with a large variety of techniques like skiing, rock climbing, abseiling/rappelling, and survival in extreme temperatures.

During the First World War (1914–1918), Italy declared war on Austria and this led to confrontations in the alpine regions of the two countries. The need for skilled mountain troops was more evident than ever before, and in 1915 this situation led to the nucleus of the first German mountain unit being deployed from their base in Bavaria to a southern part of the front where they fought with distinction. These men came mostly from the Württemberg and Bavarian Armies. None other than the celebrated Erwin Rommel (1891–1944), later leader of the Second World War German Afrika Korps, commanded a Württemberg Gebirgsjäger unit, and won the much-coveted *Pour Le Mérite* medal whilst on the Italian Front.

German mountain troops were called Gebirgsjäger or Gebirgstruppen; *Jäger* means literally 'hunter' but in the German army it designates a light infantry soldier or rifleman. The same applies to the French term 'chasseur'.

After the First World War, the Treaty of Versailles was signed in June 1919. Defeated Germany was permitted a small professional army (called *Reichswehr*) limited to 100,000 soldiers divided into seven infantry divisions and three cavalry divisions. The tiny Reichswehr was organized by Chief of Truppenamt General Hans von Seeckt who believed that one day the Versailles imposed 'diktat' would be renounced.

The Reichswehr was a professionnal army in which men voluntarily enlisted for twelve years and officers for twenty-five years. Until 1927 the Reichswehr was controlled by an Allied Commission and forbidden the possession and use of a number of weapons notably tanks, airplanes, combat-gas, heavy artillery, and automatic weapons. However these prohibited weapons were designed, researched, tested, built and experimented in secrecy abroad, notably in Russia, Spain and Sweden, while other military equipment and arms were furtively purchased in Holland, Denmark and Switzerland.

The 100,000 soldiers limit was exceeded secretly, and this part of the army was known as the *Schwarze Reichswehr* ('black army'). The official national army was completed by a number of private political militias – notably by Ernst Röhm's Nazi Sturmabteilung (SA Brownshirts or storm battalions). The bloody purge in the end of June 1934 – the massacre of the SA leadership, so-called Night of Long Knives (see Chapter 7) – allowed Hitler to eliminate all opposition within the Nazi party and to rally the regular German army to his new established regime. To demonstrate loyalty to Hitler, the Defence Minister von Blomberg ordered that 'non-Aryans' were to be dismissed from the army, and allowed the Nazi party's eagle and swastika to be adopted as part of the official army insignia.

In March 1935 the Treaty of Versailles was renounced and Hitler re-established mass conscription, which brought the armed forces up to one million. The army name Reichswehr was changed to *Wehrmacht* (defence force), which regrouped into three main arms: *das Heer* (army), *die Luftwaffe* (newly created air force) and *die Kriegsmarine* (navy).

In November 1935 a new *Reichskriegflag* (war flag) was officially introduced. Combining Nazi regalia and German tradition, it was composed of a red ground, a superimposed white cross at the junction of which was a white disc containing a black swastika; in the upper left corner of the flag was a small black iron cross.

The year 1936 marked a significant break in German economic and military strategy. With the economy slightly back to the levels of the pre-1929 crisis, and the political regime assured, Hitler was in position to start re-arming seriously, and to create an economy geared more closely to the conduct of war. In August 1936, the Four Year Plan was launched under Hermann Göring's direction. The plan was intended to prepare for war, and develop a 'blockade-free' autarkic self-sufficient economy in which materials vital for war would be produced at home instead of imported.

The organization initiated expensive investment programmes in basic chemicals, synthetic fuel oil, synthetic rubber, aluminium, and iron-ore extraction, all designed to reduce German dependence on outside sources. The plan also introduced a programme of improvement in agriculture to ensure that Germany would not be starved into submission in a future war. Simultaneously a programme of labour re-training was launched to make sure that the skilled workforce needed for a war economy would be in place. Side by side with the economic strategy, Hitler ordered a very great increase in military expenditure designed to bring the armed forces to a state of war readiness by 1940. The army itself developed plans for expansion but Hitler's programme imposed a faster pace and a larger scale. So ambitious were the plans for rearmament and economic development that neither the Army command nor the economic, and industrial managements thought them feasible.

To experiment with tactics, test new weapons and train men Hitler actively supported the rebellious nationalist general Franco during the Spanish Civil War (1936–1939). By 1937, the German army had grown to considerable size, strength and quality.

After the end of the First World War, a corps of the experienced mountain personnel was retained by the small army of the Weimar Republic. The corps was quickly re-activated by Hitler after the repudiation of the Versailles Treaty in 1935, and by then the first mountain division was created. With the annexion of Austria in 1938, many experienced mountaineers joined the German Army, sufficient to raise two new divisions.

Gebirgstruppen were infantry troops, supremely fit individuals including accomplished *Ski-jäger* (skiers), *Bergführer* (mountain guides) and *Alpinisten* (mountaineers) specially trained for combat in mountainous regions. For obvious reasons, as already pointed out, mountain troopers came from the southern mountainous parts of Germany – Wurtemberg and Bavaria – and from Austria where alpinism and mountain warfare had a long history. The Gebirgstruppen formed elite troops whose *esprit de corps* and pride were enhanced by a distinctive emblem, the Edelweiss flower introduced in 1939.

German mountain troops had two main officers who were idolized by their men: the charismatic general Eduard Dietl, the 'hero of Narvik' and the highly popular general Julius Ringel, commander of the 5th Division, nicknamed 'Papa Ringel'. Mountain troops participated in all the major campaigns and battles of the Second World War: Poland, Norway, France, Balkans, Greece, Crete and the Russian front (see Chapter 2).

As the war progressed the Gebirgsjäger – like the Fallschirmjäger (paratroopers) – were used more and more as ordinary infantry on all fronts and anti-partisan guerilla warfare units, especially in the Balkans and in Russia where elite characteristics and high-level *esprit de corps* were often stained by unsoldiery actions, blind retaliations and atrocities against civilians. Like all other German forces after 1943 the mountain units suffered many casualties and were regularly re-organized, and replenished, but the late replacements never really matched the original quality of the prior divisions.

*   *   *

The aim of this book is to provide a general survey about German mountain troops in the Second World War. Mountain troops were a specialized sub-branch of the Heer (army ground force), which was a part of the Wehrmacht.

The Waffen SS, the military force of the SS (Schutz-Staffeln or protection squads of the Nazi party) also raised several mountain formations, which are discussed in Chapter 7.

The author hopes that this volume will help modellers, collectors, re-enactors, and anyone interested in general German military topics and the Second World War to find useful information.

Disclaimer

Given the sensitive nature of the subject of this book the author insists on closing this introduction with the following statement.

The German Army and Waffen SS mountain troops, as with all other aspects of Hitler's regime, are historical subjects where claims to absolute objectivity and technical detachment sound somewhat artificial and forced – not to say dishonest. Let there be no misinterpretation: the author has no truck with attempts at apologism for Nazism or justifying Nazi crimes or encouraging any form of neo-Nazism, racism, anti-Semitism, or championing any ideology based on violence, racism, hatred and totalitarianism. This book is non-political and its aim is to provide technical and historical information about the German mountain troops during the Second World War.

Jean-Denis G.G. Lepage
Groningen
The Netherlands
July MMXXIII

Note: All measurements in this book are given in metric units.
1 millimetre (mm) = 0.039 in
1 centimetre (cm) = 0.393 in
1 metre (m) = 0.328 ft or 1.094 yd
1 kilometre (km) = 0.612 mi
1 litre (l) = 0.22 Imperial gallon or 0.26 US gallon
1 cubic centimetre (cm3) = 0.061 cubic in.
1 cubic metre (m3) = 1.308 cubic yd
1 kilogramme (kg) = 2.205 lbs
1 tonne (t) = 1.102 US ton (= 2,000 pounds) or 0.984 British ton (= 2,240 pounds).

CHAPTER ONE

MOUNTAIN WARFARE

Generalities

Extreme conditions

The Alps and the Balkan mountains were the main spots where German mountain troops operated, but combats also took them into Poland, Norway, Russia, France, Greece and Italy.

Mountains are intrinsically high, jagged, and desolate. They fundamentally include rocky terrains, spectacular snow-capped peaks, majestic summits, impressive ice fields and glaciers, deep-cut and abrupt valleys, precipitous river gorges, as well as barren plateaux, huge arid ridges, and vast expanses covered with thick forests. Mountains were – and indeed always are – a breathtaking, splendid and amazingly beautiful sight, but they are also hard, rough, dangerous, inaccessible, and inhospitable. Mountains can at times be unable to sustain the growth of trees, plants and shrubs, and the highest mountains are inadequate to support any form of life at all.

Just like jungles and swamps, they created extreme conditions for warfare making logistics and endurance more difficult than other kinds of terrain. The peculiarities of mountain terrain, such as limited routes, extreme weather conditions and difficult communications, necessitate additional considerations in the tactics employed. Mountain troops in a way, were/are similar to naval personnel in that they are fighting two forces at the same time, the first being the natural surroundings, the second opponent being enemy troops.

Mountaineering techniques vary largely on location, season and the route chosen. Mountain troops must be trained to hike and climb on all sorts of terrain including level or inclined ground, steep rock, snow and ice – each type presenting its own difficulties and hazards. In considering military operations in highlands, basic factors must be borne in mind: the slownesss of all movement due to terrain, sudden changes of weather, weariness that can quickly become exhaustion, and the difficulty of command and supply. Indeed military operations carried out in mountainous environments are always of much longer duration than in smooth and flat lands, and therefore must make proper allowance for the factors of time and space. Movements, command, and supply in mountain areas present enormous difficulties.

In such craggy, stark, remote, and sloping surroundings, every route had to be cleared of enemy observation, while defiles and bridges had to be controlled and peaks held because 'who holds the heights, holds the valley'.

People have different reactions and susceptibilities to altitude, but above 2,000–5,000m (6,600–16,400 feet), altitude may cause headache, vomiting, tiredness and dizziness to men and animals. Fortunately mountain warfare did not often take place in such extreme altitude.

Another primary danger in mountainous sites was (and still is) the sudden change of weather from clear and bright sunshine to high winds, precipitations and even storms with snow whiteouts making it difficult to follow or retrace a route.

When advancing over glaciers mountain troopers sometimes must form a rope team because crevasses pose a great hazard. Those large cracks are not always visible when covered with snow, while frost and wind might form dangerous snowbridges over them that may collapse under the weight of a man.

Mountain warfare called for and still requires infantry specialists in extremely good physical condition, with endurance and special climbing skills, equipment and techniques usually not available to mechanized forces. It also required a peculiar mental fitness, morale and patience. Indeed in winter in northern Russia, Finland and Norway daylight often amounts to only a few hours a day. Campaigning in the inhospitable Arctic regions was far from easy. The territory to patrol, conquer and control consisted of immense bare tundras, steep mountains, wide belts of trackless forests relieved only by normally impassable bogland. An operation could last for weeks, and the Gebirgsjäger endured all the hazards of ambush, storm, cold and starvation. They could lose their way and perish slowly in dense pine forested mountains, which hid sun and stars.

Soldiers operating in mountains have to take everything they need with them including supplies, food, ammunition, and other equipment, and they must take good care of those reserves as resupply might sometimes be difficult if not impossible. They had to carry weapons, equipment and supplies in cloud, snow and cold, and every ridge and every crest-line could hide an ambush or a sniper. With the constant threat of hostile weather, snowdrifts, and avalanches, as well as rockfalls and gaping ravines – not to mention enemy troops – a serious wound might often result in death as evacuation to a first aid post could take hours, even days.

Communication

By 1939 military wireless radio communications were still in their infancy, but the German armed forces were relatively advanced. Each German armoured, mountain, and infantry division included a signal radio battalion enabling successful and rapid co-ordination between ground units, artillery and aviation. The signal corps *Waffenfarbe* (colour of service) was lemon yellow/light brown. One important factor in mountain warfare was indeed command, signal and communication. Warfare among the peaks was a severe test of the skill and leadership of the junior officers, as the operations of small groups of combatants call for a high standard of training and discipline. Communications and cooperation between forces scattered over many square miles of forest, rock, snow or ice were difficult to maintain, and command problems were far more complex than in flat lowlands.

In the valleys, cyclists, motorcyclists, armoured cars and halftracks equipped with radio sets could be used for communication. But as soon as one ventured on the heights, field telephone wire laying was most difficult, so wireless radio was the primary means of communication, although among the peaks there were many dead areas where radio was unreliable and sometimes jammed by adverse weather conditions. Larger aerials were required than those used on conventional radio sets and in an attempt to improve reception, aerials were often attached to the tops of trees for greater reception. Sometimes radio relay stations were set up to combat the loss of signals in certain situations.

The Germans employed rather good technology with high power devices such as the Fu5 SE 10 or the 1.0 kW-KW ranging to about 10 km, fitted in reconnaissance vehicles, tanks or radio-trucks. The infantry portable manpack set Feld Fu A1 had a range of 1km.

However, wireless radio communications had their disadvantages. Technical difficulties were numerous, and atmospheric conditions could interfere. In the heat of battle, orders transmitted could be confused or misheard. Wireless was also entirely unsecret, the enemy tuning on the same frequency could hear all plans and possibly jam the communication. Coding and decoding machines like the Enigma cipher device slowed the communications down and did not guarantee complete security. For all these reasons, if German warfare theorists considered quick and modern transmission a primary requirement for Blitzkrieg, old ideas and outdated equipment were never completely discarded. Morse code was also still in service because a small battery-powered wireless telegraph (W/T) can transmit an audible message further than a radio telephone (R/T) transceiver.

Communications by means of runners on foot, horse or bicycle, motorbikes or even carrier pigeons were still used. Similarly, at very short range whistles and hand signals were still useful. Semaphores and heliograph, blinker, coloured rockets and smoke could be practicable at medium range. Just like at sea, a commonly used method of signalling consisted of using flags. Indeed with favourable clear weather conditions, men visible to each other could make a chain, and send signals up to miles away. Another method of signalling was carried out with the use of trained hounds and large St Bernard dogs. These strong working dogs could carry written messages and a small load of ammunition, food and medical packs. They could also be used to help with rescue duty.

Tactics

There were actually no special 'mountain tactics', however the hampering effects of deep snow, cold, sloping terrains and variations in weather greatly influenced the combat methods of normally organized and equipped infantry troops.

Scouting

As in regular infantry operations, scouts were/are soldiers sent out ahead of a main force so as to gather information about the enemy's position, strength, or movements. Time and effort spent on reconnaissance is never wasted, as obtaining intelligence is a vital process in the conduct of war. The reconnaissance units of any army require considerable specialized skills, insight and above all daring as they have the most dangerous task to do: they form the point of the advance, they must probe forwards until they encounter enemy forces, they penetrate enemy deployment where they must remain unseen in order to observe and obtain tactical intelligence; if they are located and attacked they have to evade quickly.

Gathered information such as enemy's strength, identification, intention, position, speed, direction and so on, are then transmitted to divisional headquarters who, according to their reports, send other units forwards or withdraw them. The information obtained on the organization and strength of the enemy provides the tactical basis for the conduct of a battle. Mountain scouts also had extra tasks of reconnaissance, notably information on the safety of the paths and trails, depth of snow, load capacity of iced streams, and danger of avalanches. So signs on stakes well above the snow or the marking of rocks or trees and the setting up of flags on poles were necessary to mark routes, trails and paths.

The tactics laid out on mountain warfare had to be adhered to at all times to ensure the safety of troops deployed in mountainous regions. This covered weapons, tactics, food, clothing and safety. Planning was the key to mountain survival and it was constantly stressed in military manuals. Troops must never be deprived of their freedom of action in the mountains, however difficult the terrain or inclement the weather, so careful preparation was required no matter how small the operation being undertaken.

Engineers

One of the most vital components of the German Mountain Division was its combat Gebirgspioniere (mountain engineers). Together with regular combat engineer duties the Gebirgspioniere had numerous other tasks to perform such as improving mountain passes and roads which sometimes meant rock blasting, avalanche blasting and the draining of water from mountain roads. Mountain troops must have adequate food, water, ammunition and special equipment to complete their tasks. As just discussed, keeping a mountain unit on the move was vital but often extremely difficult, so various means were employed by Gebirgspioniere to ensure that they could.

Cable lines, which could support loads between 150 kg and 500 kg were constructed for moving men and equipment up and down along steep slopes. A difference in height of 400 metres was required for the descent, and they could span an area of one kilometre. Engineers could also establish a so-called *via ferrata* (Italian for iron path) known in German as *Klettersteig* (climbing path), that was a prepared route made of pegs, carved steps, iron pins, hand hooks, ropes or steel cables, fixed lines, ascenders, iron rungs, or ladders anchored in steep or vertical rock on which mountain troopers could advance, progress, or climb in relative safety. *Via ferrata* were of great help in ensuring troops could move and occupy high and dominating peaks where observation posts could be sited and light artillery positioned. These artificial aids in highly exposed terrain could be permanent, semi-permanent or temporary.

Where no roads or paths existed or were in bad condition, new ones had to be constructed to allow the passage of motorized units and pack trains. Mountain engineers had to carry out the bridging of iced surfaces and torrents, bridge protection and maintenance against ice, and the blasting of the frozen surface of marshes. Engineers had to prepare mule trails, and the construction of aerial cableways. They would establish pontoons, trestle or improvised bridges for crossing torrents, streams and rivers.

Other activities included road maintenance, demolitions, reconnaissance, water supply and water purification, and sometimes fighting, as well as erecting or destroying barbed wire fences. Another important task was laying and detecting mines (both anti-personnel and anti-tank) as well as placing and/or neutralizing booby traps. Protection against snow and the clearing of snowed-in roads and trails would be part of the engineers' work as well as the construction of defensive positions. Bridges were often needed and engineers were required to construct various types ranging from simple rope footbridges for infantrymen, to heavier pontoon bridges able to support pack trains, armour, artillery and vehicles. The G-Gerät, for example, was a kit that provided the components to build a simple footbridge of 120 metres in length, a 4-ton suspension bridge capable of supporting motor vehicles and horse drawn carts or a 2-ton inflatable boat bridge which could span 60 metres.

The B-Gerät was another kit, which enabled the construction of an 8- to 16-ton bridge supported by pontoon ferries. The K-Gerät was very useful in that it enabled the construction of a 20m long 16-ton bridge without assistance in only 20 minutes. Obtaining building materials from rock and blasting pathways through solid rock was sometimes required and explosives, detonators, both electric and cordite fuse were used. Powersaws, flame-throwers and other specialist building/demolition equipment were used for the construction of mountain strongpoints and safety installations, which contained snow fences and avalanche deflectors to guard against rock falls and avalanches.

On the march the eventual changes in weather necessitated the use of some form of shelter, which on most occasions had to be constructed by hand. These could range from simple hastily constructed shelters made from the ice or natural caves, which were sometimes found in mountains. Other shelters such as lightweight canvas tents were widely used for bivouacs. There were also Finnish plywood light shelters that could be broken down and transported providing effective windproof protection. In base camps, where timber would be available log cabins were also constructed and often proved quite sufficient in keeping out the harsh mountain weather. Illumination inside these shelters was vital and provided either by candles, oil or paraffin lamps, or battery-fed electric torches and lamps.

Advancing

Thanks to scouts and engineers, the main troops could advance. Mobility to carry out a march in the mountains was often the basis for a successful operation. If possible the enemy had be surprised, and surprise was more likely if the troops avoided predictable tracks and trails, and moved across terrain which was considered impassable. Marching, advancing and fighting in mountainous areas was difficult, to say the least. Because of the limited number of trails and the numerous natural obstacles, advancing was greatly slowed down due to fatigue, and troops generally marched in smaller units than was customary on flat lowland terrain. The maximum practical formation was a battalion or a company, if possible reinforced with a reconnaissance platoon and engineers pushing forward to help clear the trail.

The exact size was, of course, determined by the nature of the mission. A division in small self-sustaining units minimized the risk of ambush, and each column could fight independently. To prevent small bodies of snipers from holding up the advance, mountain reconnaissance called for the marking of trails followed by pack transport, where the path should be improved, and where the progression could not be exposed to enemy observation.

When possible light guns or machine guns were placed near the head of the column. Both stationary flank guards and mobile patrols were thrown out to secure high positions ahead and to the flanks. These elements rejoined the column as it passed. Where the climbing was particularly stiff, the infantry mingled with the artillery and pack train to help when necessary. Supplies and artillery moved at a very slow walking pace. The skill and leadership of junior commanders was severely tested in mountain warfare. Indeed, forces generally were split into small groups, and advancing columns were often dispersed in large areas and impassable terrain. Since lateral communication was often very difficult, command of deployed units became much more complicated than over level terrain, and efficiency required a high standard of training and discipline.

The appearance and nature of a landscape could change quickly and considerably, for example under a sudden cover of snow or in fog. Orientation points could be non-existent. It was thus of vital importance to constantly have a full knowledge of one's own position and determine the exact direction for advancing. Depending on visibility, cardinal directions could be determined by the position of the sun, and NCO and officers were equipped with maps, as well as lensatic compasses whose magnetized pointers indicated the direction of magnetic north.

Movements over mountains were thus slow and required a lot of consideration and meticulous anticipation regarding food, clothing and route planning. Preparation, it must be repeated, was vital for any operation as most mountainous areas at the time lacked an adequate road network and consideration had to be given not only to troop movements, but also for the ease of supply by pack animals and the transportation of heavy equipment.

Avalanches also proved to be a real and constant threat in high mountains, and careful map reading and particular attention to weather forecasts was vital as it could allow troops to avoid a dangerous area or pass through it with the least danger. To minimize the risk of avalanche, careful spacing at 30 metre intervals of men in columns, light zigzagging was undertaken. Each group made it to safe ground and the next group then moved off to the safe area. Permanent tracks could be protected by vertical wooden snow fences. In a sparsely wooded zone timber fences could be replaced with temporary snow walls made of snow or ice-blocks. Vertical ascents or descents were not always allowed due to the risk of dislodging snow or pieces of rock.

Ice crossing too was a very dangerous affair. First of all, one had to measure the thickness and evaluate the carrying capacity of the ice. One could put down layers of twigs, straw, or freshly cut small branches and also sprinkle the slippery surface with moss, grass, small-grained sand, gravel or small pieces of rock – if available in the vicinity.

Advancing in a mountainous environment is exhausting, and regular pauses are needed. Short rests without removing packs were of little use, but rest-halts (if possible in areas protected from the wind and the sun) of three or four hours to permit the unloading of both men and animals were regularly taken. However as opposed to normal mountain practice and depending upon the weather, halts had to be short when the temperature was low, reducing the time the men were exposed to cold and wind.

At night troops would establish a temporary bivouac in a site as much protected and camouflaged as possible. Sentries (frequently relieved) and patrols maintained continuity of observation and the safety of the troops. Aside from tactical requirements the selection of the bivouac site must as much as possible offer some kind of protection against damp, wind and cold. The nearness to a supply of wood for fuel, and fresh water was of course desirable. The type of bivouac construction depended upon several factors: the envisaged length of occupancy; the weather and temperature; the local situation; the material and equipment available. Tents could be pitched and primitive branch shelters, earth or turf huts, or lean-to windbreaks built. Foliage, moss, straw (when available) could be used to make beds, but all extra time spent on construction shortened the time available for rest, but ensured better relaxation and added warmth later.

Ski Warfare

Snow presents many drawbacks as it affects and often complicates human living and economic activities, but it has also many advantages, which could be exploited by the military. Snow, when properly employed, could provide shelter against cold and wind, yet it is porous enough to permit ventilation. When thickly packed, it could afford protection against enemy small calibre fire, and it is also a good camouflage material. However shelters and combat positions were not as easy to camouflage as may be assumed, as dug-up snow looks very different to undisrupted snow. Another advantage was that snow forms a loose surface on which sporty people, winter tourists and soldiers can quickly glide downhill or cross-country with planks attached to their feet. Skiing for transportation purposes seems to have been used as early as 5000 years BC in China and

The metal badge was worn on the left side of the field cap by skiing experts of the German mountain troops.

Russia, and about 3000 BC in Scandinavia. The use of skis was always a part of mountain warfare. In 1767, military ski competitions appeared combining cross-country skiing and rifle shooting. This practice later evolved into a typical northern European winter sport known as the biathlon. In the period 1807–1814 during the Napoleonic Wars, ski warfare was employed in the conflict opposing Denmark-Norway to Sweden. As already discussed, in the second half of the nineteenth century three European nations came to the fore with specialized mountain infantry and ski troops: The French Chasseurs Alpins; the Italian Alpini; and the Austro-German Gebirgsjäger.

The First World War (1914–1918) with a front opposing Italy to Austria in the Alps saw a tremendous development of mountain warfare and ski troops became an integral part of it. Skiing troops played a key role in the successes of the Finnish war effort against the Soviet Union during the Winter War in 1939. During the war opposing the Soviet Union to Nazi Germany (1941–1945) German Gebirgsjäger and Soviet ski troops were widely employed in remote forested terrain with no roads and sub-Artic tundras. Ski warfare even extended to the Middle East where the Australian Ski Corps were deployed against Vichy French forces in the mountains of Lebanon. The Second World War also saw the appearance of the United States Army 10th Mountain Division especially created and trained for mountain and ski combat, which fought in Italy.

Attack

The Second World War brought forth a number of élite infantry units such as airborne and paratroopers, assault engineers and mountain troops. However the infantry's traditional roles persisted: to seize and hold ground and to deny ground to the enemy. Even in modern post-Second World War warfare, it was still the possession of the land, the conquest of enemy territory that decided the issue in a battle. The possession of ground is the visible sign of victory, and occupation is a guarantee of the exercise of complete control.

The most significant German innovation in the period 1939–41 was *Blitzkrieg* (lightning war). This new tactic basically consisted of concentrating mobility in armoured and mechanized divisions. Blitzkrieg was a swift, and sudden offensive by combined tank and infantry forces supported by artillery and aviation. It was actuated by dynamic command and control through wireless radio and rapidly laid line communication, simultaneously with paratroopers dropping, and air attacks upon enemy airfields, lines of communication and resistance centres. German Blitzkrieg achieved brillant successes in 1939–1941 in Poland, Denmark, Norway, Netherlands, France and the Balkans. But when the Nazis invaded the USSR in June 1941, Blitzkrieg at first provided tremendous successes but it failed after a while because, for the first time, German logistics were unable to maintain their momentum to sufficient depth to achieve ultimate victory.

Obviously, Blitzkrieg could not be used in mountain warfare, and mountain troops had to perform offensive actions without or with only limited support from armoured vehicles, heavy artillery and aviation. 'Fewer heavy weapons and more ammunition' was a German principle in mountain warfare.

There was naturally no strict standard procedure for attacking, as every situation required an adequate tactical plan, but there were general guidelines. Assembly areas, in view of the difficulty of movement in mountains, were generally further forward than normal. Deployment was often delayed until contact with the enemy was made, and ski troops were valuable for reconnaissance as well as for sudden and surprise attack. Since normal units used as reserves only had limited mobility in deep snow, the Germans employed ski troops for reserves wherever possible. These ski units were used for immediate counter-attacks, which were directed where possible against the flank of the enemy. The Germans also used the ski troops as raiding parties for harassing the enemy's front and rear. As a rule, limited objectives only were possible, but combined frontal and flank attacks as well as encirclements were made whenever possible.

Commanding high positions were seized early in the action. Indeed the early possession of dominating heights was essential for the security of forces moving in the valleys. According to many factors, the main attack would generally follow the valleys, as they alone gave freedom of movement to a strong force and its supply trains. Ordinary artillery support fire was sometimes found of little value. Particularly in attacking uphill with artillery support, there was danger of rockslides caused by the shells of the covering fire. Howitzers and mortars with their high trajectories were often most effective. Downhill attack was easier for assault troops, but presented tactical and ballistic problems for artillery. Ranges of weapons are usually underestimated in clear weather and overestimated in fog. At low temperatures, weapons at first fire short. When visibility was bad, ammunition consumption rose, as many rounds were wasted. Since ammunition supply presented a difficult problem in mountain warfare, the usual German procedure was to fire only on orders. Single rounds were aimed with the greatest care, for considerations of economy as well as effect.

To prevent surprise, or deal with surprise attacks, support weapons were dispersed. Using their expertise in broken-country combat, mountain soldiers would ascend a rocky slope making use of any available cover. In doing so they saved their ammunition for the final attack when it would be more effective than if they had fired up hill at enemies under cover. Finally they would rush and assault the top of the ridge with impressive self-control and determination – at least that was in theory.

Combat in forested mountains

When attacking in forested mountains, the Germans usually divided the area into company sectors and first deployed reconnaissance patrols to discover and estimate the weakest enemy position. Then companies would advance usually in wedge formation and creep forward up to close-combat range, always keeping contact with adjacent and supporting units. The companies then would storm the enemy's position using hand grenades, pole charges, and close-combat weapons. According to circumstances, commanders then decided whether to roll up the enemy position on the more important flank or to hold the ground until reinforcements would arrive before continuing the offensive.

In order to neutralize enemy (treetop) snipers and ambushers, the Germans fired bursts of automatic weapons rather than single shots. They often considered fighting in forested environments as the primary task of riflemen and machine gunners, since the employment of support weapons like mortars or artillery pieces was difficult. When they had to cross a large clearing within the wooded area, the attacking party would work themselves close to the edge of the trees. Then under sustained machine-gun fire they would simultaneously rush, jump, and crawl seeking whatever cover was available.

Defence

There were in fact no special mountain tactics for defence, as every battle demanded adequate adaptation, but there were a few guidelines too. In defence it was better to have only the foremost defence areas on, or in front of, the crest and to have the support weapons on the rear slope. Well-placed mines could start rockslides.

It must be remembered that obstacles and field fortifications took much longer to build in deep snow or frozen ground than in normal terrain. Indeed the difficulty of organizing a defensive position with outposts and strongpoints with all-round entrenched defence in deep snow or on frozen ground always took a considerable time. Besides, transporting and positioning weapons like artillery necessitated the building of paths, tracks and roads, and camouflage was particularly stressed under such adverse conditions.

When strong outposts were required, the construction of defensive positions – which might also provide essential shelter against the weather – was very often difficult if not impossible in hard rocky terrain. Indeed cover was often minimal. Whereas a regular infantryman could dig a small foxhole, or a slit trench or a dugout, a mountain trooper could not always have the benefit of such a luxury. Often high winds prevented conventional sheltering forms being constructed. So simple parapets made of loose stones acting as windbreaks were constructed behind which men could try to sleep. Pieces of rocks could sometimes form a kind of shelter in the shape of a *sangar* – a small protecting structure made of piled rocks and stones. However during combat this form of primitive shelter or cover could sometimes backfire on the occupiers, with bullets and shells chipping off razor sharp lumps of rock, which in some cases could be just as dangerous as bullets or shell splinters. Packed or frozen snow and piles of ice blocks could be employed as a material for protection against light fire weapons. They required no revetting but frozen hay, grass, straw, timber, tree branches (when available) were sometimes used to support trench walls, and weapon emplacements, and to provide additional insulation in shelters.

In retreat, every single avenue of pursuit was blocked or mined, if possible forcing the pursuers to storm high crags in the face of delaying fire. Demolition operations to blast roads or cover them with avalanches were particularly effective. One could also withdraw under cover of fog and follow the edge of it up the mountainside. However, among the high peaks, according to experienced mountaineers, fog was apt to be unreliable cover.

Logistics & Transport

Vehicles

German Second World War mountain troops were basically light infantry, with a very specific training adapted to the environment in which they would operate. When operating in high mountains, they could not rely upon the supporting forces available to ordinary infantry including transport trucks or halftracks, heavy artillery, armoured reconnaissance vehicles, tanks, and aviation. Flexibility was the watchword among mountain officers and great responsibility was placed on junior officers. One foul up could result in catastrophe for the whole detachment. Flexibility was again important when it came to transportation and sometimes whatever was at hand would be pressed into service.

In high mountain warfare vehicles were virtually useless. They could only be used in the valleys and on prepared tracks, and under relatively fair weather conditions. Even so at temperatures under zero Celsius the use of tanks and motorized equipment was limited. Snow was a tank obstacle when higher than the vehicle's ground clearance. Tractors could negotiate snow slightly over a foot deep, but motorcycles were useless at six or seven inches. Petrol consumption at very low temperatures was calculated to be five times normal. Snow-fighting equipment such as curved upright blades, rotary ploughs, and similar machinery was included in the German materiel in winter. During a short break, vehicles were placed radiator to radiator, and a tarpaulin would be thrown over the hoods in order to keep the engines warm. During a lengthy halt, vehicles were pulled off the road, and placed into deeper snow, which obviously had to be dug away from the wheel tracks to prevent possible stalling. In all cases, when possible, they were parked in forested spots or bushes for camouflage purpose.

As the war went on, the Gebirgsjäger experts were more and more deployed as regular infantry on all the fronts. Then they would be partly motorized – at least when adequate vehicles were available in sufficient number.

Indeed Second World War German armies had well-designed, high quality military vehicles including motorbikes (with or without a sidecar), cars, vans, light, medium and heavy trucks, ambulances, and buses. For off-road and cross-country movement they had halftracks, 4-, 6-, and 8-wheeled reconnaissance cars, and all-wheel drive trucks, as well as self-propelled guns and tracked armoured combat vehicles. However these vehicles were always in limited numbers and generally allocated with priority to the elite *Panzer* and *Waffen SS* motorized divisions. Motorization of the normal light and regular infantry divisions – even during the victorious beginning of the war – was much less modern and abundant than the propaganda asserted. Actually full motorization of German infantry was never totally achieved. Horses (and mules) were used in enormous quantities, not only by mountain troops but also by all Army formations right throughout the war, mainly behind but also in the front line.

Bicycles

German mountain divisions sometimes included a Fahrrad Abteilung (Cyclist Battalion). In the 1930s many European armies raised bicycle troops. This would seem curious, odd and ridiculously old-fashioned today but the importance of the bicycle as military troop transportation must not be underestimated. Western Europe offered a dense network of relatively good metalled roads. Under favourable conditions bicyclists could cover long distances; with regular breaks, on flat land, dry weather and a good road, an average speed of 20 km/h may be easily sustained.

A troop on bicycles could approach a fighting zone quietly for a surprise attack – much quieter than a horse-mounted cavalry unit or a column of vehicles anyway. It could be instantly deployed for combat without the services of horse-holders. Bicycles are cheap devices requiring none of the specialist care and supply of horses (food, water, veterinary care etc) or of motorized vehicles (fuel, maintenance etc).

It should be noted that bicycles were extensively used as transport by the Vietnamese force in the Indochina/Vietnam wars from 1946 to 1975. Disadvantages were however numerous. These included the muscular strain imposed on the cyclists, the limited load that each bicyclist could carry, the total absence of protection (as much from weather as from enemy fire), and the fact that such a troop was always bound to a flat, smooth, and metalled road or path. Nonetheless, the German Wehrmacht made a wide use of the cheap *Fahrrad* (bicycle) as mean of transportation all through the Second World War. In the cavalry, for example, one squadron per regiment was formed of men mounted on bicycles. Wehrmacht bicyclists generally used the standardized German-made M1939 Patria WKC bicycle, but also many other German brands, and foreign cycles were captured and used.

Pack Animals

The term pack animal is usually employed in contrast to draught animal, which is a working animal that typically pulls a load behind itself (such as a cart, or a sled) rather than carrying goods directly on its back.

Lorries, cars, halftracks and armoured vehicles were widely used in the valleys and where practicable mountain roads existed. But when it came to offroad/cross-country and steep climbing, vehicles were useless. Then pack animals (such as horses, ponies, donkeys and mules) were employed to transport supplies, heavy weapons and ammunition. In Lapland domesticated reindeers were employed, and in the Caucasus, Bactrian camels and small donkeys were pressed into service. The weights these animals could carry were quite considerable. While an average man could carry a load from 45 to 75 pounds, horses and mules could take burdens up to 200 pounds. The authorised strength of a typical German mountain division might consist of 13,000 men, and a detachment of pack animals for supply purposes in difficult terrain, which could number around 5,500–6,000 animals, 700 horse drawn vehicles and 1,400 motor vehicles (including cars and motorcycles).

Mountain troops' collective equipment (machine guns, artillery, and mortars, ammunition, food, water, radio sets and radio batteries, and all other bulky stores) was thus carried in difficult terrains by pack animals – particularly mules. The mule (the offspring of a male donkey and a female horse) was one of the favourite mountain pack animals. The mule has the patience, endurance, sure footedness, sense, and drought tolerance of the donkey, combined with the size, speed, strength and courage of the horse. Indeed mules show more patience under the pressure of heavy weights. Their skin is harder and less sensitive than that of horses, rendering them more capable of resisting sun and rain. Mules are stronger and require less food than horses. Their hooves are harder than horses', and they show a natural resistance to disease and insects.

Mules and all other pack animals gave mountain troops a flexibility they badly needed. Many animals were issued to the German Army but civilian horses and transports were commandeered as well.

Animals were also used for draught use – that is pulling waggons, carts and sleds. In winter and mountain warfare sledges were often substituted for most wheeled vehicles. The German mountain troops used several light sleds of standard width pulled or drawn by harnessed men or draught animals. Troops operating in high-altitude mountains were issued the so-called *akjas*. Adopted from the Finns, the *akja* was a small, wooden canoe-like sled on skis used to carry dismounted guns, machine guns, and other heavy supply loads. The weapon could be fired from the sled. The *akja* sled pulled by two or three harnessed men could also be used for evacuating wounded and sick soldiers.

Based on German, Russian and Finnish experiences, mountain troops and formations deployed on the Russian front in winter were issued standard sleds. The Army sled No.1 had a carrying capacity of 300 kg (661 lbs), the No.3 500 kg (1,102 lbs), the No.3/1 Ambulance sled could carry two lying wounded or four sitting casualties, and the No.5 1,000kg (2,205 lb). These sleds – drawn by one or more animals – could transport a light gun, a small field kitchen, a few personnel or a load of supplies. Mountain troops also used larger animal-drawn sleds, like the *troika* or the *panje* used in Russia. They provided a vital form of transport, which supplemented horse-drawn carts, as well as wheeled and tracked vehicles. So in high mountains or during the winter months on the Russian Front animals were often the only means of moving, supporting, and supplying troops in the field. Artillery supporting pieces could also be installed directly on ski or sled runners.

However, the use of pack animals also had disadvantages. They were of course much more vulnerable to gunfire and explosions than mechanical vehicles. Many horses, ponies and mules were killed in all theatres of war, and many were rendered unserviceable on account of wounds or sickness. Animals need to rest, sleep, drink and eat (fodder sometimes needed to be taken along). Although a mule or horse are much less noisy then motorized vehicles, the animals' sudden braying could inadvertendly reveal their position to the enemy, representing a serious security problem in combat zones.

Animals needed significant support such as veterinary surgeons and specialist personnel for exercising, leading, feeding, washing, brushing, grooming, as well as keeping clean and in working order all equipment related to the animals. Men driving animals also had to be extremely careful with loading, saddling and packing; particularly they must avoid unbalanced or poorly tied loads that would rub the animals' back sore, or that would cause the loss of valuable supply if falling off. Therefore several harnessed carrying appliances were designed in the form of wooden framed packsaddles, containers of all kinds, or large baskets attached with ropes and leather straps.

Air Support

Flying among peaks and between steep-sided valleys at night was often difficult and sometimes impossible. During daylight in unstable weather it was always daunting, and particularly dangerous in bad weather with strong winds, snowstorms, fog and clouds. It can easily be imagined how difficult it must be to fly, reconnoitre, identify friends and foes, as well as carrying out accurate level bombing, dive-bombing and strafing. For supporting mountain troops, airplanes were often useless, but when conditions allowed they could be extremely helpful for providing intelligence and reconnaissance, and of significant assistance for parachuting men or dropping ammunition and supplies to isolated units. Provided there was a flat practicable airstrip in the vicinity, supplies, re-inforcement, and support weapons could be flown by airplanes and gliders, but both take-off and landing in a mountainous site always remained risky operations.

An important mission for airmen was evacuating wounded and sick, thus saving casulties prolonged and painful journeys by stretchers down rough sloping tracks and precipices. Specifically for use in mountain warfare, several German standard airplanes could be fitted with *Schneekufen* (skis). For example the small, STOL (Short-Take-Off-and-Landing), low-weight, reconnaissance and liaison airplane Fieseler Fi 156 Storch (English: stork) was widely used by the Germans for its ability to take-off and land

Siebel Fh-104 Hallore with ski. The Siebel Fh-104, designed by engineer Hans Klemm, was a small transport, communication and liaison aircraft which could take five persons including the pilot. Powered by two Hirth HM 508C inverted-vee air-cooled engines, the aircraft had a maximum speed of 217 mph. Some 48 units (all unarmed) were produced and used in the communication/transport role.

on primitive and very short runways in harsh conditions. The biplane recon/bomber/trainer Heinkel He45, the two-engined medium liaison Siebel Fh-104 Hallore, the reconnaissance two-engined and double beam Focke-Wulf Fw189 Uhu, and even the heavier tri-motor transport Junkers Ju 52 could also be equipped with skis for use in mountains and in winter.

Food

Basic German Army Food

During the Second World War national standards of diet varied greatly and food was extremely various, depending on many factors. Gradually strangled by blockade, the Axis powers' diets declined as *Ersatz* (substitute) food became more common. In non-combat conditions, Army regulations stipulated coffee, bread and jam for breakfast. A warm meal was served at noon with soup, boiled beef, pork, cabbages and potatoes. Dinner, served about 18.00, consisted of a warm soup and cold food (bread, canned sardines, dry sausage, black pudding and so on). German doctors considered it unhealthy to drink while eating and one's thirst was quenched after the meal.

Compared to the well-fed British Tommy and the vitamined American GI, the German private was rather poorly provided for, certainly after 1943. In combat conditions, large groups of men campaigning for long periods in difficult terrains made feeding difficult. Many a unit suffered starvation and lack of vitamins resulting in diseases (e.g. scurvy, beriberi) and a decrease of health and morale. Depending on conditions, it was more or less difficult to provide regular hot meals and fresh vegetables. Eating out of tins was not always appetizing and the variety of tinned food was limited and monotonous. The official daily ration scale for a German Army soldier in the field in 1941 comprised one loaf of bread (650 grams), butter or fat substitute (45 grams), Wurst (sausage 120 grams), fresh meat (210 grams), jam (200 grams), real coffee (60 grams), coffee substitute (100 grams). This ration scale could not always be adhered to and considerable variations occured including extras when available – especially from home – such as chocolate and liquor. After 1943 foodstuffs, but also clothing and other supplies, were often stolen or taken out of necessity. Captured food, plundered supplies and hunted game ameliorated regular military food. Statistics clearly showed that the weekly ration of bread, meat, fresh vegetables, and fats was greatly decreased in the last phase of the war.

Alcohol was officially prohibited but soldiers always managed to smuggle wine and brandy. The German army authorities strongly warned against the use of alcohol as protection against cold. In fact alcohol dilates the pores and merely simulates a short feeling of warmth. It abets exhaustion, and must never be taken prior to physical exertion. Strong liquors like schnapps, cognac or vodka could be consumed when taken in hot beverages like coffee or tea, and only allowed if a subsequent relaxed stay in heated accomodation was expected, for example at night in the bivouac or in winter quarters.

Regarding smoking, German soldiers were issued various brands such as Der Artikel cigarettes or Feiner Bulgarischer tobacco. Turkish tobacco and American smokes were eagerly sought, stolen from prisoners and purchased in the black market, but it should be noted that the Nazi regime, and Hitler in the particular, was violently anti-alcohol and anti-smoking. As early as June 1940 Hitler had ordered tobacco rations to be distributed to the military 'in a manner that would dissuade' soldiers from smoking. Cigarette rations were limited to six per man per day, with alternative rations for non-smokers (chocolate or extra food). Cigarettes were available for purchase, but these were generally limited to 50 per man per month, and often unavailable during times of rapid advance or retreat. Tobacco rations were denied to women and youths serving in Wehrmacht auxiliary roles. The impact of these and other measures (for instance, medical lectures to discourage soldiers from smoking) was arguably rather limited. A 1944 survey of 1,000 soldiers found that the proportion of servicemen smoking had increased.

Specific mountain supplies

In mountain warfare, careful consideration had to be given to food. Naturally the emphasis was on foodstuffs with a high calorific value but which did not occupy much space nor weigh too much. High calories were required to provide energy for the constant marching and climbing, which burnt many calories. If not quickly replaced a lack of calories could result in fatigue and lower alertness, which could prove disastrous in warfare in a mountain region. The colder the weather, the more fat must be included in the food. Field rations also had to be able to be eaten raw or cooked as quickly as possible. This was due to the fact that at high altitude food took longer to be cooked and as a result required more fuel, thus adding weight to carry along. Dried meats, canned food, dehydrated vegetables and biscuits proved the best for these conditions, although on shorter operations chocolate, grape sugar or dried fruit were also practical.

The German Army had several types of field ranges, field bakeries, dough mixers, ovens, stew kettles, boilers, and other mobile collective cooking equipment placed on trailers or on vehicles. A popular and widely used apparatus was a horse-drawn rolling field kitchen known as *Gulaschkanone* (goulash gun) with various capacities – large for feeding 125 to 225 men, and small for 50 to 125 men. Such facilities could not always be used by mountain troops on operation, so Gebirgsjäger were issued portable ration heaters. These were small gasoline stoves, weighing a little over a pound. The stove worked by burning vaporized gasoline, but it had no pressure pump. Pressure was built up by heating the burner with petrol or fuel tablets burnt in a small cup below the tank and maintained by the heat generated by the stove itself. More widely issued were fuel tablets, the commonest of which was Esbit: tablets of hexamethylehe tetramine. The fuel was packed in a paper carton, which was carried in the fuel-tablet stove (Esbit Kocher).

Fodder

Another factor that had to be considered was foodstuffs for the pack animals, which under normal circumstances would have been grass or hay provided by Mother Nature. At high altitude, however, that kind of food was available scarcely or not at all, so grain and dried fodder in the form of cattle cake and other substitute foodstuffs had to be brought along, which complicated logistical problems.

Chapter Two

Historical Background

The Second World War

The Second World War between 1939 and 1945 remains the most deadly and geographically the most widespread military conflict the world has ever seen. Although the fighting reached across many parts of the globe, most countries involved shared a united effort aimed at ending the aggression of the Axis Powers – Germany, Italy, and Japan.

Unlike many wars, blame for outbreak of the Second World War can be firmly placed in the hands of a single individual, Adolf Hitler, Chancellor of Germany from 1933. His programme for power was set down in his book *Mein Kampf* ('My Struggle') written in part while he was in jail after a failed attempt to overthrow the Weimar Republic in 1923. In his book Hitler outlined his vision of a future in which all Germans would be united in a single Reich including notably Austria, the Sudentenland in Czechoslovakia, as well as parts of Poland.

Once he came to power, Hitler immediately began a programme of rearmament, at first hidden, but eventually openly. He ordered the organization of the Germany economy on a war footing, and soon started to realize his aims. First was the reoccupation of the Rhineland, which was forbidden by the Treaty of Versailles. In March 1936 German troops marched across the Rhine bridges, but the French did not react. Once in the Rhineland, Hitler was able to order the construction of the West Wall, a system of fortifications that severely limited any French ability to attack Germany if her eastern allies were threatened.

Hitler next moved to Austria, which was bloodlessly annexed in March 1938. Then he quickly turned his attention on Czechoslovakia, where the presence of three million Sudeten Germans, once part of the Austro-Hungarian Empire, gave him an excuse for intervening. Under intense pressure from their apparent allies, Britain and France, the Czechs were forced to give in (29 September 1938), and hand over the Sudentenland.

In 1939, Hitler targeted Poland. This time Danzig and the Polish Corridor were his excuse. His first attempt, in March, was rebuffed by strong Polish resistance and joint English and French support of the Poles. Hitler had a deadline of September for military action, and he spent the summer building up to his invasion, and deploying his forces on the Polish border. Finally, after a fabricated incident at the frontier, Hitler invaded Poland on 1 September 1939. On 3 September, both France and Britain declared war on Germany.

The Second World War had begun.

German Mountain Troops After 1918

After the First World War, the restrictive Treaty of Versailles from 1919 limited the German army to a defensive force named the Reichswehr comprising 100,000 professional soldiers. After 1933, when Hitler came to power and rejected the limitations of the Treaty of Versailles, an expansion of the army took place, and by then the small existing mountain unit was developed too. Recruits for this formation were at first drawn from the mountain-trained Bavarian State Police and placed under the command of General Ludwig Kübler. A Mountain Brigade was formed in August 1937 under the command of General Hubert Lanz. This brigade went on to constitute the 1st Gebirgs Division, the unit on which subsequent German mountain divisions were formed.

When Germany annexed Austria in 1938, their armed forces were absorbed into the German order of battle, and as a result two new divisions were created – the 2nd and 3rd Gebirgs Divisions. The 2nd Mountain Division was raised by a former Austrian officer, Valentin Feurstein and based around Austrian alpine and infantry battalions; its recruiting areas were Vorarlberg, Tyrol, Salzburg and Upper Carinthina. In 1938, those mountain units were involved in the invasion of the Sudetenland (western border of Bohemia-Moravia in former Czechoslovakia). After this region had been annexed, mountain troops had another area for training.

Poland

German mountain troops participated in many Second World War battles, not only as specialist troops in the highest peaks of Norway, in the Alps, in the Caucasus, the Balkans and Greece, but also as regular infantrymen fighting in Russian swamps and tundras, and in the burning desert of North Africa. On the whole they earned a high reputation for bravery in attack and steadfastness in defence.

The invasion of Poland by Nazi Germany on 1 September 1939 marked the beginning of the Second World War. The German invasion had been prepared by the non-aggression Molotov–Ribbentrop Pact between Germany and the Soviet Union. German forces invaded Poland from the north, south, and west. On the first day of the attack, massive air raids disrupted the Polish Air force, while fast moving Panzer units cut through the thin Polish border defences. Bombing of the railways and airbases cut all lines of communication, while the rapidly advancing armies left clusters of isolated Polish troops to be picked off later. As the Wehrmacht advanced, Polish forces withdrew from their forward bases of operation close to the Germany–Poland border to more established defence lines to the east.

Rapidly the Germans gained an undisputed advantage, and Polish forces then withdrew to the south-east where they prepared for a long defence while awaiting expected support and relief from their Allies, France and Britain. Those two countries had alliance pacts with Poland and had declared war on Germany on 3 September. In the end their aid to Poland never came. On 17 September, the Soviet Red Army invaded Eastern Poland, rendering the Polish plan of defence useless. Attacked on two fronts at the same time, Poland was doomed. On 6 October, German and Soviet forces gained full control over Poland dividing and annexing the whole country.

Both the 1st and 2nd German mountain divisions and elements of the 3rd division were involved in the Polish campaign. Attacking in the south, they secured the Dukla Pass in the Carpathian ridge. Then they advanced in an eastern direction in difficult terrain to the provincial capital of Galicia, the city of Lemberg, which was an important hub for both road and railroad communications. They encircled the garrison, and held their position against Polish counter-attacks for six days. The invasion of Poland by the Soviet Union from the east broke the will of the Poles to resist any longer, and the Lemberg garrison capitulated.

After the successful invasion of Poland, German mountain troops were transferred back to Germany.

Norway

The next German attacks were aimed at Denmark and Norway. Germany's main iron ore supply came from Sweden. During the summer ore could be shipped down the Baltic Sea, but during the winter it had to be shipped from the Norwegian coast. The British wanted to control northern Norway around the port of Narvik, and occupy the Swedish steel areas, as part of a plan to go to the aid of Finland, then under attack by Russia. Hitler decided to pre-empt this by attacking Norway, and taking Denmark on the way. The Danes offered no resistance to the Germans, and Denmark fell in a single day, 9 April 1940, after only token fighting. Norway was different. The Norwegian campaign in April 1940 opposed German forces to Norwegian troops, supported by a British and French expeditionary force (about 38,000 soldiers).

Elements of the German 2nd Mountain Division, headed by General Eduard Dietl were shipped to the port of Narvik. On 9 April 1940 they captured the port without serious opposition, but things went badly wrong one day later when the British Navy launched a counter-attack disembarking numerous French, British, Polish and Norwegian troops. General Dietl's force was trapped in Narvik, put under considerable pressure with ammunition running short. Although reinforcement in men and supplies were parachuted in, the German mountain troopers' situation became critical. The beleaguered men were ultimately saved when the German troops attacked France. The Franco-British Allies withdrew their forces in early June 1940.

The campaign ended with the occupation of the whole of Norway by Germany. However, the Norwegian government, King Haakon VII, and a few exiled forces managed to escape to London where they continued the war against Nazi Germany until 1945.

France

The Battle of France, also known as *Fall Gelb* (Case Yellow) started in early May 1940 with the invasion of the Netherlands and Belgium intended to attract the French mobile forces and the British Expeditionary Force (BEF) to the North. Simultaneously German armoured units made their main surprise, fast, and audacious offensive through the Ardennes forested ridge, outflanking the French border fortifications of the Maginot Line and then advancing along the Somme valley. Then, they cut off and surrounded the Franco-British Allied units that had moved into Belgium to meet them. British,

Belgian and French forces were pushed back to the sea by the German armies, and pocketed at the port of Dunkirk. Fortunately the British managed to evacuate their Expeditionary Force (Operation Dynamo). Then the rest of the dispirited French army was defeated by the German combination of air superiority and armoured mobility pushing deep into France. The invaders seized Paris without a fight on 14 June 1940. After the collapse of the French Army, and negotiations ending the hostilities, Northern France was occupied, and Southern France became a puppet state (known as the État Français – aka Vichy regime – because the capital was the spa city of Vichy) headed by the aged Marshal Philippe Pétain (1856–1951).

During the Battle of France the 1st German Mountain Division advanced along the Maas (Meuse) Valley, then reached and crossed the heavily defended Aisne Canal on 5 June. After fierce combat against French units and French colonial troops, the 1st Mountain Division rushed and crossed the Marne River on 11 June. Right afterwards, the division was transferred to the southern part of the front near Lyon for reducing French pockets of resistance. Before they could reach those positions, the French capitulated and agreed to sign an armistice. Then the 1st division was tasked with occupation duties on the Franco-Swiss border region.

The newly formed 6th Mountain Division was deployed in France but arrived too late to take an active part in the combat. It was then used for occupation duties in France.

The 1st German Mountain Division was picked out to participate in Operation Sea Lion, the planned but never carried out invasion of the United Kingdom in the summer of 1940. The 1st Division was also selected for another aborted offensive (Operation Felix): the capture of Gibraltar in Southern Spain planned in the summer of 1940 but also never carried out.

The Balkans and Greece

After the tremendous German victories in the West, the United Kingdom was badly mauled but undefeated, and Prime Minister Winston Churchill vowed to continue the war declaring: 'We shall defend our island, whatever the cost may be. We shall fight on the beaches, we shall fight on the landing-grounds, we shall fight in the fields and in the streets, we shall fight in the hills. We shall never surrender!'

By then Hitler was preparing his ultimate and grandiose aim: the invasion and destruction of the Soviet Union. However in October 1940, much to his surprise and annoyance, his ally Fascist Italy started the invasion of Greece. In the early months of 1941, Italy's offensive had stalled and a Greek counter-offensive pushed Italian Fascist forces back into Albania. Hitler decided to delay the invasion of the USSR and come to the rescue of his repulsed and humiliated ally instead. So the unexpected Balkan campaign started.

Germany rapidly deployed troops in Romania and Bulgaria and attacked Greece from the east. Meanwhile, the British landed troops to aid the Greek defences. Suddenly a coup d'état in Yugoslavia in March 1941 caused Hitler to intervene in that country too. The invasion of Yugoslavia by Germany and Italy started on 6 April, simultaneously with renewed attacks on Greece. The 5th and 6th Mountain Divisions (together forming XVIII *Gebirgskorps*) were tasked to attack the heavily defended Greek Metaxas fortified line, a mission carried out with success after heavy fighting against the determined Greeks.

Then the 6th Division fought its way down south towards Corinth in the Greek Peloponnese. Meanwhile the 1st and 4th Mountain Divisions took part in the invasion of Yugoslavia, facing stubborn opposition, and covering on foot long distances in adverse mountain countryside in bad weather. On 11 April Hungary joined the invasion, and by 17 April the Yugoslavs were overwhelmed, defeated, and forced to sign an armistice. By 26 April Athens was seized, and by 30 April 1941 all of mainland Greece was under German and Italian control. By then, all British forces were evacuated to Crete, and later withdrawn to Egypt. After the unexpected Balkan campaign, all four *Gebirgsdivisions* involved on that front were withdrawn for rest and refit.

Crete

The next major involvement of para- and mountain troopers in Greece was the invasion of Crete. The fifth largest island in the Mediterranean and the largest of the islands forming part of modern Greece, Crete is relatively long and narrow, stretching for 160 miles (260 km) on its east-west axis and varying in width from 7.5 to 37 miles (12 to 60 km). The administrative centre is Heraklion (previously called Candia). Because of its strategic situation halfway between Greece and Libya, Crete represented an important operational base from which to carry on the war in the Eastern Mediterranean and North Africa.

For this reason Germany invaded Crete by air on 20 May 1941. The Battle of Crete opposed defending Greek, British and Commonwealth troops to a large attacking force of German paratroopers. However the attack had been badly prepared as the assault troops were not provided with maps, and intelligence sources had underestimated the strength of the defenders, and wrongly pinpointed the defenders' strongholds. After one day of fighting, the German paratroopers had suffered heavy casualties and the Allied troops were confident that they would repulse them. However, the next day, through communication failures, Allies' tactical hesitation and German offensive operations, Maleme airfield in western Crete was seized. This move allowed the Germans to land the 5th Mountain Division by air and by sea. This reinforcement came at the right time, and enabled the Germans to retake the initiative. Although they suffered heavy casualties in bitter fighting, paratroopers and mountain troopers managed to overwhelm the defensive positions on the north of the island. Then they advanced relentlessly, forcing the Greek and Commonwealth Allied forces to withdraw to the southern coast. By 1 June 1941, after rearguard actions, the Royal Navy evacuated many Commonwealth and British soldiers, although many were captured while some escapees joined the Cretan resistance.

Later during the Second World War, the German troops encountered serious armed opposition from partisans supported by the civilian population. The occupation of Crete evolved into a costly guerilla war, and as a response the Germans routinely executed partisans and civilians in retaliation. In a spiral of violence civilians were rounded up randomly in local villages for reprisal executions, such as at the massacres of Kondomari and Viannos. Right after the war, two German generals were tried and executed for their roles in the killing of 3,000 of the island's inhabitants.

After the challenging battle of Crete the 5th Mountain Division was allowed a period of rest, but the war was not over. Then with the Balkan Penisula, Greece and Crete conquered, Hitler could at last turn his full attention to his main goal: attacking the USSR.

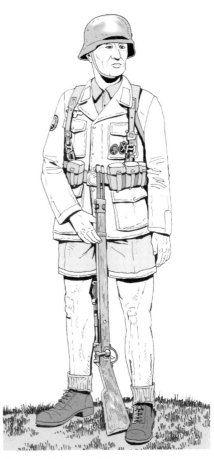

The Battle of Crete was the first time in military history when paratroopers were used en masse. Due to the number of casualties and the belief that airborne forces no longer had the advantage of surprise, Adolf Hitler became reluctant to authorise further large airborne operations, preferring instead to employ paratroopers as elite ground troops. The Allies on the contrary were so impressed by the potential of surprise attacks from the sky that they started to develop in earnest their own para/airborne assault forces.

During the Battle of Crete, mountain troopers were issued with lightweight cotton summer clothing, which replaced their regular warm fieldgrey wool uniforms.

German aims

Nazi Germany and the Soviet Union had signed a treaty of non-aggression in August 1939, only for temporary political, economic, and strategic purposes – actually crushing Poland. However it was clear from the start that war between the two dictatorially led countries would break out one day. Indeed Hitler and the German High Command started planning an attack on the Soviet Union as early as July 1940. Given the ultra racist, expansionist and aggressive character of the Nazi ideology, conquering the USSR was a crucial necessity. According to Hitler's concept of *Lebensraum* (living space) defined in his 1925 book *Mein Kampf,* the immense fertile lands in Ukraine, Belarus and western Russia had to be conquered, repopulated by German and Germanic people, and exploited for the sole benefit of Nazi Germany. As for the native local Russian population, some of them were to be kept as forced slave labour, while millions were to be exterminated or deported to Siberia. The Nazis planned to create four Reichskommissariats: Ostland (Estonia, Lithuania, Latvia, and Byelorussia aka White Russia); Ukraine (southern Russia); Moskau (northern Russia); and Kaukasus (Transcaucasia).

Events, however, took a different course.

Barbarossa and the Russian Front

The invasion of the USSR had been suspended by the resolute and successful British resistance in the summer of 1940 during the Battle of Britain, and delayed because of the Balkans imbroglio. At last, in the spring of 1941, Hitler believed he could quickly overwhelm the USSR. Operation Barbarossa was the code name for the Axis invasion of the Soviet Union, which was launched on 22 June 1941. It was a huge offensive marking a decisive escalation from a European war to a World War.

At first owing to surprise, Soviet unpreparedness, and Blitzkrieg tactics, the German advance was triumphant with a great number of casualties inflicted on the Soviet troops, many Russian armies were defeated and taken prisoner, as well as large territories conquered and occupied, notably the most important economic areas of the Soviet Union in Ukraine, parts of Ruthenia, and Belarus. However with the coming of the terrible Russian winter, the offensive bogged down right in front of Moscow. The failure of Operation Barbarossa at the end of 1941 reversed the fortunes of the Third Reich, as the Russians were badly mauled but not defeated at all. The subsequent Soviet winter counter-offensive stopped their advance. The Germans had overconfidently expected a quick collapse of Soviet resistance as in Poland and France. However the Soviet Red Army took on the Wehrmacht's strongest strikes, and henceforth forced them to an exhausting war of attrition for which Nazi Germany was totally unprepared.

Indeed from early 1942 to mid-1944 the Eastern Front became an enormous theatre of operations, in which more forces were involved than in any other theatre of war in history. The area saw some of the Second World War's most gigantic clashes, most horrendous atrocities, and highest losses in human lives (for both Soviet and Axis forces alike). The Russian Front had enormous consequences for the outcome of the Second World War and the ensuing history of the second half of the twentieth century.

German mountain troops on the Southern Sector of the Russian Front

First and Fourth Mountain Divisions formed XLIX Gebirgs Korps at the time of Barbarossa in June 1941. They marched into Russian-held Polish territory passing Cracow, then smashing through the Soviet border fortified 'Stalin Line', and starting a long advance eastwards into southern Russia during the summer and autumn of 1941. They forced the Red Army back over the River Bug at Vinnista, and pushed them back into the pocket of Uman. They continued their victorious advance to Berislav near the Sea of Azov, and marched to Tokmak, Diakowo and Taganrog.

Released during the winter of 1941–42, 1st and 4th Divisions were engaged in the Caucasus Mountains in the summer of 1942, where a detachment climbed Mount Elbrus (5,663m high). By then the German troopers – short of supplies and severely weakened – faced strong Soviet counter-attacks. After fierce combats, they were withdrawn and transferred to the swamps of the Kuban bridgehead for rest and refit. They defended that area until the second half of 1943, and by October 1944 the 4th Division was forced to retreat back to Hungary. As for the exhausted 1st Division, it was withdrawn from the Russian Front in March 1943 and elements were deployed in the Balkans, and other units transferred to Hungary until December 1944.

Mountain troops in the Northern Sector of the Russian Front

When Operation Barbarossa was launched, the German 2nd and 3rd Mountain Divisions (forming together Gebirgskorps Norwegen) were engaged in the most inhospitable climate in the sub-artic northern sector of the front, and tasked with capturing the port of Murmansk. At first their advance was rapid and successful, but due to extremely adverse conditions, unpassable terrain, over-extended supply lines, and determined Soviet resistance, the repeated offensives in that sector failed. In the winter of 1941–42, the 3rd Division was withdrawn from the front and replaced with the 6th. Together the 2nd, the 6th and the 7th Army Mountain Divisions, reinforced with the 6th Waffen SS Mountain Division 'Nord' formed the XVIII Mountain Corps commanded by General Schörner. Numerous protracted, repeated, and ferocious combats took place on the Murmansk front with both the German and the Soviet forces only reaching exhaustion and a costly stalemate throughout 1942 and 1943.

Meanwhile, after the battle of Crete, the 5th Mountain Division was involved on the Leningrad front in April 1942, notably in the Volkhov pocket, and in fierce battles around Lake Ladoga in the summer of 1943.

It should be noted that in November 1942 Mountain Regiment 756 was transferred to Tunisia in North Africa and attached to the 334 Infantry Division to defend the road to Tunis against the British.

Gradually, the Wehrmacht's harassed, diminished and exhausted forces could no longer attack along the entire Russian Front, and subsequent operations to retake the initiative and re-conquer Soviet territories failed. After the long and bitterly fought battle and siege of Stalingrad (August 1942–February 1943) ended in a crushing defeat, and the failed counter-offensive at Kursk (Operation Citadel in July–August 1943), the Finnish withdrew from the conflict in mid-1944, and concluded a separate peace with the USSR. By then under renewed massive Russian offensives, the Eastern Front gradually collapsed. As a result all German forces, including the mountain divisions fought desperate defensive and rearguard actions, but were inexorably forced to retreat in a western direction.

By mid-1944 large parts of the USSR were cleared of German troops and the Red Army approached Central Europe and the Balkans. Following the Vistula-Oder offensive in January-February 1945 they entered Germany and captured Berlin after a battle that lasted from 16 April to 2 May 1945.

The Western Front

Battle of the Bulge

German mountain troops were neither engaged during the 6 June 1944 D-Day landing, nor the Battle of Normandy in the summer of 1944, nor Operation Dragoon – the 15 August 1944 Allied invasion of Southern France between Toulon and Cannes, but they took part to Operation Nordwind, which was a part of the Ardennes Offensive in the winter 1944–45.

The German Ardennes Offensive – aka *Wacht am Rhein* ('Watch on the Rhine'), aka Battle of the Bulge – was Hitler's last gamble. This ultimate massive German offensive in the West lasted from 16 December 1944 to 25 January 1945. The ambitious and somewhat unrealistic aim of the offensive was to attack through the mountainous Ardennes, and swing north to capture the port of Antwerp. By splitting the American and British armies, Hitler hoped to weaken and defeat them, thereby forcing them to negotiate and sign a peace treaty. Once victory was achieved in the West, Hitler would then concentrate all his remaining armies against the Soviet Union in Eastern Europe, and consequently win the war – at least that was his idea.

The attack was initially successful owing to surprise and bad weather, but it was soon repulsed by an Allied combined air and land counter-attack, which eventually brought the depleted German forces back to their starting points.

Operation Nordwind

German mountain troops, notably elements of the 6th Waffen SS Mountain Division 'Nord', and units of the 2nd Mountain Division were involved in the second, smaller offensive (Operation Nordwind) into Alsace that started on 1 January 1945. Aiming to recapture Strasbourg, and relieving the pressure in the Ardennes after the failure of the Battle of the Bulge, they attacked the Allies at multiple points. Because the Allied lines had become severely stretched in response to the crisis in the Ardennes, stopping and repulsing the Nordwind offensive was a costly affair that lasted almost four weeks. However that operation, too, was doomed to end in failure for the Germans. The culmination of Allied counter-attacks restored the front line to the area of the German border and collapsed the Colmar Pocket.

Retreat and collapse of the German mountain forces

By early 1945 Nazi Germany was on the point of total military disintegration. On the Eastern Front, the Soviet Red Army advanced through Poland, crossed the Oder River between Küstrin and Frankfurt-an-der-Oder, started the invasion of Germany, and prepared for the last battle: the seizure of Berlin, the capital of the Third Reich.

Meanwhile on the Western Front the Germans had lost the Ardennes Offensive. Soon British and Canadian forces had crossed the Rhine and invaded the German industrial heartland of the Ruhr. In the meantime American armies in the south had captured Lorraine, crossed the Rhine River, and were moving towards Mainz and Mannheim. In the South, the American, British and Commonwealth forces heavily pressed the German armies in Italy, and obliged them to retreat behind the Po River and withdraw into the foothills of the Alps.

In late 1944 and early 1945, fragmented remnants of the Gebirgsjäger fought numerous last-ditch battles, and rearguard actions against the Allies in Austria, Southern Germany, Silesia, Slovakia, Northern Italy and Norway, but to no avail. In early May 1945, Nazi Germany was defeated and all German forces surrendered.

In the meantime the Führer Adolf Hitler had committed suicide on 30 April 1945 in his bunker under the Chancellery in Berlin.

CHAPTER THREE

ORGANIZATION OF THE GERMAN ARMY MOUNTAIN DIVISIONS

Companies and battalions

R anks and units in Army mountain divisions were the same as those of the regular German infantry. The smallest unit was a *Gruppe* (squad) of ten *Jäger* (literally 'hunters' but usually translated as riflemen) commanded by a *Gefreiter* (corporal). Three or four *Gruppen* formed a 30 to 40 men strong *Zug* (platoon) commanded by Unteroffizieren (NCOs – Non-Commissioned Officers). Three or four *Züge* (platoons) comprised a *Kompanie* (company) of between 90 and 160 soldiers (an average complement of 147 men was common). The company, usually equipped with 12 machine guns, one anti-tank rifle and two 8 cm mortars, was commanded by an Oberleutnant (lieutenant) or a Hauptmann (captain). In the Waffen-SS, the company was called a *Sturm*.

Three or four companies constituted a Bataillon, also called Abteilung commanded by a major or an Oberstleutnant (lieutenant colonel); the standard make-up of a battalion was about 900 officers and men, but this, too, could vary somewhat. In the Waffen-SS, the Bataillon was designated Sturmbann headed by a Sturmbannführer (lieutenant colonel).

Regiment

Three or more mountain battalions with various service and support companies formed a mountain regiment commanded by an oberstleutnant or Oberst (colonel). The regiment, comprising between 2,000 and 3,000 men, was a mixed combat force, which could be engaged alone. A brigade, often synonymous with regiment, was a mixed formation composed of various units engaged independently or attached for serving within a division.

It generally included a headquarters with intelligence service, sometimes a mounted platoon, an engineering platoon, several anti-tank and anti-aircraft artillery companies (or one artillery bataillon) and usually three infantry battalions.

In the Waffen-SS, the regiment was called Standarte, and headed by a Standarteführer (Colonel).

Combat group

A division (or a regiment) was sometimes too large to be positioned for a surprise attack or a local operation. Therefore according to the requirements of a specific battle, elements could be re-assembled to constitute temporary, smaller, flexible, and multi-armed formations designated *Kampfgruppen* (combat groups) often called after the commander's name. In the last phase of the Second World War, *Kampfgruppen* were also formed with survivors of various decimated units, which were hastily regrouped together.

Division

Several regiments/brigades and various support units formed a Gebirgsdivision (moutain division), placed under the command of a Generalmajor (division general) or a Generalleutnant (general).

In the German army, a mountain division was a light infantry unit usually with a simpler organization and smaller complement than a regular infantry division. It included a headquarters, two Gebirgsjäger light infantry regiments (each with three battalions, sometimes only two), one mountain artillery regiment (equipped with mortars, light anti-tank, anti-aircraft and mountain guns), a Gebirgspionierbataillon (engineering battalion), one Aufklärungsabteilung (a reconnaissance unit); a Nachrichtenabteilung (signal unit), and Divisions Einheiten (service units). In addition each Gebirgsjägerdivision could include a battalion of Panzerjäger (anti-tank guns or motorized self-propelled anti-tank guns), a bicycle battalion, a motorbike battalion, and a pack mule/horse transport battalion. However, the composition of a division was variable, and many divisions, particularly those raised in the last phase of the war, did not always conform to normal army regulations.

Corps and Army Group

During the Second World War mountain divisions and SS mountain divisions – like regular Heer infantry and Panzer units – could be organized and operate as part of a larger body called Gebirgskorps (mountain corps). This large managerial and administrative unit included two or three divisions, and had a permanent co-ordinating staff and various support units such as transport, signals and military police. Designated by Roman figures, the following mountain corps were established: the XV Gebirgskorps, the XVIII Gebirgskorps, the XIX Gebirgskorps, the XXI Gebirgskorps, the XXII Gebirgskorps, the XXXVI Gebirgskorps, the XLIX Gebirgskorps and the LI Gebirgskorps. The Waffen SS mountain divisions comprised the V SS-Gebirgskorps, and the IX SS-Gebirgskorps.

Two, three or four Army Corps formed a Heeresgruppe or an Armeegruppe (HGr. army group) headed by a Generalfeldmarschall (General of the Army/Field Marshal).

Ranks

German mountain troops had on the whole a rather close tie with their commanding officers, probably because junior officers, NCOs and lower ranks have shared the same difficulties, hazards, suffering and adversities together. Commanders often took a unique and fatherlike interest in the welfare of their troops, and senior officers like Julius Ringel and Eduard Dietl were extremely popular. However there were also brutal, strictly disciplinarian, intolerant, merciless, hated and unpopular officers. Field Marshal Ferdinand Schörner for example was a committed Nazi, who did not hesitate to sacrifice his men, and who ordered atrocities and war crimes against civilians.

Nevertheless mountain troopers were often commonly appreciative of their leadership, proud of their corps, and appreciative of their accomplishments.

German Second World War mountain troops had the same ranks as the regular Heer infantry, with a few small differences: notably a private was called a Jäger and a senior private an Oberjäger. Ranks were shown on collar patches, on shoulder straps, on headgear, and on various insignia and badges worn on tunic sleeves.

The table below shows the German mountain trooper ranks and their approximate equivalents in the US Army.

Gebirgsjäger	Mountain trooper
Oberjäger	Trooper 1st Class
Gefreiter	Acting Corporal
Obergefreiter	Corporal
Hauptgefreiter	Corporal
Unterfeldwebel	Staff Sergeant
Fahnrich	Staff Sergeant
Feldwebel	Technical Sergeant
Oberfeldwebel	Master Sergeant
Hauptfeldwebel	First Sergeant
Stabfeldwebel	Staff Sergeant
Leutnant	Second Lieutenant
Oberleutnant	First Lieutenant
Hauptmann	Captain
Major	Major
Oberstleutnant	Lieutenant Colonel
Oberst	Colonel
Generalmajor	Brigadier General
Generalleutnant	Major General
General der Gebirgstruppen	General
Generalfeldmarschall	Field Marshal

German mountain NCO.

The German Army Mountain Divisions

Between 1938 and 1945 eleven Heer (army) mountain divisions were raised, as well as several improvised formations, and *Kampfgruppen* (combat groups), which were sometimes designated 'divisions' but which were well under regular strength. Although some mountain troops were involved in atrocities against civilians and committed war crimes, the German mountain divisions are often militarily regarded as 'elite' formations. It should be noted that the Waffen SS also formed especially trained mountain divisions. These are discussed in Chapter 7.

1st Gebirgsdivision

The 1st Gebirgsdivision was formed in April 1938 in Garmisch (Bavaria). Composed of Germans and Austrians, the unit was successively commanded by:

General der Gebirgstruppen Ludwig Kübler (1 September 1939–25 October 1940)

General der Gebirgstruppen Hubert Lanz (25 October 1940–17 December 1942)

Generalleutnant Walter Stettner Ritter von Grabenhofen (17 December 1942–18 October 1944)

Generalmajor August Wittmann (19 October 1944–December 1944)

Generalleutnant Josef Kübler (27 December 1944–10 March 1945)

Generalleutnant August Wittmann (17 March 1945–8 May 1945).

In 1939, the 1st Division included:

- 98th Mountain Infantry Regiment (3 Battalions);
- 99th Mountain Infantry Regiment (3 Battalions);
- 100th Mountain Infantry Regiment (3 Battalions), this regiment was transferred to the 5th Mountain division in 1940;
- 4th Panzerabwehr (anti-tank) Battalion;
- 79th Mountain Artillery Regiment (4 Battalions); as well as 54th Signals Battalion; 54th Pioneer Battalion; and 54th Supply and Service Troops.

The 1st Gebirgsdivision took part to the invasions of Poland in 1939, the Low-Countries and France in 1940, and Yugoslavia in early 1941. In summer 1941 the 1st Mountain Division was engaged on the eastern front and saw combat in the Uman pocket, Kiev, Stalino and on the Dnieper River. In 1942 the division was engaged in the Donetsk area and in the Caucasus Mountains until 1943. After the disaster of Stalingrad the division was sent to Greece for actions against partisans until April 1944. After combats in Hungary at the end of 1944, the 1st Gebirgsdivision was renamed the 1st Volks-Gebirgsdivision, and was captured by the Soviet forces in Austria in the spring of 1945. The 1st Division's emblem displayed a wreath of leaves around a white shield containing a thin black cross. Another emblem was an Edelweiss flower.

German Mountain troops were distinguished by an Edelweiss flower. This distinctive Alpine troops' symbol had been established in 1907 by the Austrian-Hungarian Emperor Franz-Joseph I (1830–1916). Leontopodium nivale (aka Edelweiss) is a mountain flower belonging to the daisy or sunflower family Asteraceae. The plant is rather rare and short-lived, and it only grows in mountain rocky limestone places at an altitude of about 1,800–3,000 metres (5,900–9,800 ft). Because of its scarcity, beauty and purity associated with the Alpine air, it has been used as a symbol for alpinism since the nineteenth century, and adopted by Austrian and German mountain forces in the 1930s.

2nd Gebirgsdivision

The 2nd Gebirgsdivision was raised in 1938 in Innsbruck (Austria) mainly from Austrian Tyrolian recruits. The unit's successive commanders were:

Generalleutnant Valentin Feurstein (1 April 1938–4 March 1941)
Generalleutnant Ernst Schlemmer (4 March 1941–2 March 1942)
Generalleutnant Georg Ritter von Hengl (2 March 1942–23 October 1943)
Generalleutnant Hans Degan (1 November 1943–6 February 1945)
Oberst (Colonel) Hans Roschmann (6 February 1945–9 February 1945)
Generalleutnant Willibald Utz (9 February 1945 – German capitulation in May 1945).

In 1939, the 2nd Division had a similar composition as the first including two infantry regiments, one artillery regiment, a cyclist battalion, one anti-tank battalion, one engineering battalion and one signal battalion.

The 2nd Division participated in the Narvik campaign (Norway) in support of the 3rd Gebirgsdivision. In June 1941 the unit was engaged on the Russian front, in Murmansk where it stayed and fought until late 1944. Badly mauled in the Russian winter offensive 1944–45, it was re-organized in February 1945 and engaged in combats in the Moselle and Saar regions. Finally the remnant of the 2nd Division retreated in southern Germany where it surrendered to the American forces in May 1945.

The 2nd Mountain Division's insignia represented a buck's head on a yellow background.

3rd Gebirgsdivision

The 3rd Gebirgsdivision was formed after the *Anschluss* (annexation of Austria) by merging the former Austrian 5th and 7th Mountain Regiments.

The 3rd Division was placed under the leadership of Generaloberst Eduard Dietl (1938–14 June 1940)

General der Gebirgstruppe Julius Ringel (14 June 1940–23 October 1940)
General der Gebirgstruppe Hans Kreysing (23 October 1940–10 August 1943)
Generalleutnant Egbert Picker (10 August 1943–26 August 1943)
General der Infanterie Siegfried Rasp (26 August 1943–10 September 1943)
Generalleutnant Egbert Picker (10 September 1943–29 September 1943)
Generalleutnant August Wittmann (29 September 1943–3 July 1944)
Generalleutnant Paul Klatt (3 July 1944–8 May 1945).

Its composition was roughly the same as the 1st and 2nd divisions (basically two mountain infantry regiments, one artillery regiment and several service battalions).

In 1939, the Austrian unit was engaged in the Polish campaign and spearheaded the offensive in Norway in April-June 1940 taking Narvik and Trondheim. In 1941, the 3rd Gebirgsdivision participated in the invasion of Russia in the northern sector (Murmansk) and then in the southern sector where it took part in the vain attempt to relieve the encircled 6th Army in Stalingrad in late 1942. After defensive battles in Ukraine, Hungary, Czechoslovakia and Upper Silesia, the 3rd Gebirgsdivision surrendered to the Soviet forces in May 1945.

After 1940, the divisional insignia represented the Narvik medal.

4th Gebirgsdivision

The 4th Gebirgsdivision was formed in 1940 with recruits from Germany and Austria. The unit's successive commanders were:

Generalleutnant Karl Eglseer (23 October 1940–1 October 1941)
Oberst Karl Wintergerst (1 October 1941–November 1941)
Generalleutnant Karl Eglseer (November 1941–22 October 1942)
Generalleutnant Hermann Kress (23 October 1942–12 August 1943)
Generalleutnant Julius Braun (13 August 1943–6 June 1944)
Oberst Karl Jank (6 June 1944–1 July 1944)
Generalleutnant Friedrich Breith (1 July 1944–23 February 1945)
Oberst Robert Bader (23 February 1945–6 April 1945)
Generalleutnant Friedrich Breith (6 April 1945–8 May 1945).

The 4th division was composed of:

Gebirgsjäger-Regiment 13
Gebirgsjäger-Regiment 91
Gebirgs-Artillerie-Regiment 94
Panzerjäger (anti-tank)-Kompanie 94
Gebirgs-Pionier (engineering)-Bataillon 94
Aufklärungsabteilung (recce) 94
Nachrichten (signal)-Abteilung 94
Gebirgsjäger-Bataillon 94
Divisions-Einheiten (service) 94.

The unit was part of the forces invading Yugoslavia and Russia. It saw combat actions on the Volga River, Uman and Caucasus. After battles in Novorossisk and Dnieper Bend, the 4th Gebirgsdivision retreated into Hungary, in the Carpathians moutains, Czechoslovakia and Austria where survivors capitulated in May 1945.

The emblem of the 4th Mountain Division displayed a stylized blue gentian flower on a light grey shield 23mm × 12 mm. It was worn next to the Edelweiss badge on the side of headgear.

The 5th divisional emblem (25 mm × 10 mm) displayed a stylized roe deer/mountain goat standing on a three-peaked mountain-top.

5th Gebirgsdivision

The 5th Gebirgsdivision was raised in the autumn of 1940 in Salzburg (Austria) predominantly with Bavarian and Austrian recruits. The 5th Division was placed under the leadership of the popular General Julius 'Papa' Ringel (1 November 1940–10 February 1944); Max-Günther Schrank (10 February 1944–18 January 1945); Hans Steets (18 January 1945–8 May 1945).

The division took part in the invasion of Greece and together with *Fallschirmjäger* (paratroopers) the seizure of Crete in May-June 1941 (Operation Merkur) where it suffered heavy losses. After rest and restructure in 1941, the 5th Gebirgsdivision was engaged on the Russian front serving in the Volkhov region and Leningrad. In December 1943, the division was transferred to Italy. The division was implicated in the Grugliasco massacre, Piedmont, alongside the 34th Infantry Division, where, on 30 April 1945, 67 civilians were executed. The unit fought delaying battles, before retreating northwards to the French Alps where it surrendered to the US Army near Turin in May 1945.

6th Gebirgsdivision

The 6th Gebirgsdivision was raised in June 1940. The unit's successive commanders were:

Generalmajor Ferdinand Schörner (1 June 1940–1 February 1942)
Generalleutnant Philipp Christian (1 February 1942–20 August 1944)
Generalmajor Max-Josef Pemsel (20 August 1944–19 April 1945)
Oberst Josef Remold (20 April 1945 – capitulation in May 1945)

As of June 1940 when it was created, the division was composed of:

141st Gebirgsjäger Regiment
143rd Gebirgsjäger Regiment
118th Mountain Artillery Regiment
112th Reconnaissance Battalion
47th Panzerjäger Battalion
91st Pioneer Battalion
96th Signals Battalion
91st Divisional Support Unit.

The division served in occupation duties in 1940–41 in France and Poland. Some elements took part in the campaign of Greece and Crete in 1941. In September 1941 the 6th Gebirgsdivision was shipped to Norway, and saw action in the Russian northern sector in the Murmansk region. After withdrawal from Norway, the 6th Gebirgsdivision surrendered to the British Army in April 1945. Its insignia displayed a yellow stylized Edelweiss on a green background.

7th Gebirgsdivision

The 7th Gebirgsdivision was formed in 1940. The unit was successively commanded by:

General der Gebirgstruppe Rudolf Konrad (1 November 1941–19 December 1941)
Generalmajor Wilhelm Weiss (19 December 1941–1 January 1942)
General der Artillerie Robert Martinek (1 January 1942–1 May 1942)
Generalleutnant August Krakau (1 May 1942–22 July 1942)
General der Artillerie Robert Martinek (22 July 1942–10 September 1942)
Generalleutnant August Krakau (10 September 1942–8 May 1945).

The 7th Mountain Division was composed of:

206th Gebirgsjäger Regiment (3 battalions with one motorized mountain Panzerjäger company)
218th Gebirgsjäger Regiment (3 battalions with one motorized mountain Panzerjäger company)
99th Panzerjäger battalion
99th Reconnaissance battalion
79th Mountain Artillery Regiment (4 battalions)
99th Mountain Pioneer Battalion;
99th Mountain Signal Battalion;
54th Mountain Feldersatz (Reserve) Battalion
54th Ski Battalion
99th Supply Troops.

The 7th Mountain Division's insignia showed a shield with a kind of cartoon-styled *Bergschuh* (mountain boot).

The 7th Division served in Russia in the winter of 1942–42 after which it was withdrawn and re-organized in Germany. In early 1942 the 7th Gebirgsdivision was sent back to the front in Finland and remained in this sector until 1945 when it retreated to Norway and surrendered to the British force at the end of the war.

8th/157th Gebirgsdivision

The 8th Gebirgsdivision was raised in 1942 in Norway with several units of the 157th infantry division. Commanded by Generalleutnant Paul Schricker, the 8th division is not believed to have reached full strength. In theory it should have been composed of:

Gebirgsjäger Regiment 296 (3 battalions)
Gebirgsjäger Regiment 297 (3 battalions)
Gebirgs Artillery Regiment 1057
Feldersatz (reserve) Battalion 1057
Panzerjäger Battalion 157
Reconnaissance Battalion 1057
Gebirgs Pionier Battalion 1057
Gebirgs Signals Battalion 1057
and Division Supply troop 1057.

The emblem of the 8th Mountain Division displayed a stylized climbing mountain soldier in a blue cloth shield. Another identification badge showed a monk holding a beer mug when the unit was redesignated 157th Mountain Division.

Parts of this unit saw action in France, notably in the anti-guerilla operation against the *Glières maquis* in the Alps (January-March 1944). The 8th Mountain Division was renamed 157th Mountain Division in August 1944, and shipped to Italy where it participated in the disarmament of the Italian army in the Po Valley. It surrendered in Italy to the US forces in April 1945.

9th Gebirgsdivision

The 9th Gebirgsdivision never fully came into existence. It was the designation allocated (perhaps by accident) to two small units in early May 1945 in the very confused situation at the end of the war.

The first 9th 'division' was in fact an ad hoc combat group named Kampfgruppe Mathias Kräutler after its commander's name, also known as Nord (North) or Special Purposes Division 140. It was formed in Lapland from various troops retreating through Finland.

The short-lived Kampfgruppe Kräutler surrendered in Norway to the British in spring 1945.

The other 9th 'Gebirgsdivision' too, was not actually a proper division but merely a mixed combat group called Kampfgruppe Raithel after its commander Colonel Helmut Heribert Raithel. This unit was also known as Ost (East), and also called Kampfgruppe Semmering as it was hastily formed in early May 1945 to defend the Semmering Pass in Austria. This Kampfgruppe was raised from various decimated units, mountain artillery schools and even Navy and Luftwaffe ground personnel. Lucky survivors of Kampfgruppe Semmering were captured by the Americans, while others much less fortunate were taken prisoner by the Russians.

1st Ski-Jäger Division

The 1st Ski-Jäger Division was created on the Russian front in late 1943. The successive commanders were:

Günther von Manteuffel, 1 April 1943–September 1943
Martin Berg, 13 May 1944–2 August 1944
Gustav Hundt, 3 October 1944–15 November 1944.

Originally the unit was a brigade, and it was expanded to the strength and status of a division in mid-1944. It was composed of Ski-Jäger Regimenten 1 and 2, and various miscellaneous existing depleted support units (notably the 18th Heavy Rocket Launcher Battalion, the 270th Assault Gun Battalion, and 152nd Tank Destroyer Battalion). The division was engaged on the Russian front in summer 1944 as part of Army Group Centre. It fought defensive battles in the Vistula region, and retreated to Czechoslovakia and Poland where survivors surrendered to the Soviet Forces in May 1945.

The emblem of the 1st Ski-Jäger Division displayed a ski placed upon three oakleaves.

118th Gebirgsdivision

The 118th Reserve Gebirgsdivision was created in late 1940. Originally it was not a combat formation but a reserve and training unit based at Innsbruck (Austria) intended to form mountain personnel. In late 1944 some staff were hastily drafted to form a Kampfgruppe (combat group). The unit saw limited security duties and anti-partisan actions in Northern Italy, and in the Balkans before being annihilated in the collapsing Eastern front in early 1945. At the end of the Second World War, survivors surrendered in Istria. The 118th's commander was Generalleutnant Wilhelm von Hösslin who was condemned for war crimes in Yugoslavia and hanged in Ljubljana in August 1947. The

118th's emblem displayed a stag head with horns or a deer outline on top of stylized peaks. Another emblem displayed three oakleaves.

High mountain battalions

The German mountain troops also included four *Hochgebirgsjäger* (high mountain) battalions created in 1942–43. They were intended and trained to fight in very extreme conditions on the highest peaks. Some high mountain battalions took part in operations in the Caucasus – the elevated mountain system and region lying between the Black Sea (west) and the Caspian Sea (east); notably the Mount Elbrus – altitude 5,642 m (18,519 ft). No further operations were launched in such extreme high conditions, and the four Hochgebirgsjäger were engaged in frontline battles as ordinary infantrymen. Battalions 1 and 2 saw action in Russia, and Hochgebirgsjäger battalions 3 and 4 were deployed in Italy, notably in the Monte-Cassino battle. As there was no real need for such highly specialized units, the four Hochgebirgsjäger battalions were disbanded in mid-1944, and their trained officers and men distributed piecemeal to the other mountain divisions.

Recruitment & Training

Men selected for the mountain divisions at first were drawn on a geographic basis, obviously from mountainous regions of Austria and Bavaria in southern Germany. Clearly this presented the advantage of providing experienced men who had a good insight into mountainous terrain and all the knowledge that it entailed. During the later stages of the war, men from other army formations were drafted or transferred to Gebirgs units with the intention of being trained as mountain troops. Although some became good soldiers, they could not always gain the years of experience that seasoned Jägers had gathered from a very early age in their mountain towns and villages.

The pay scales for mountain troops were similar to those for all other German units. The few Gebirsjäger operating in North Africa were accorded a front line premium called *Front-Zulage*.

To make the best use of weapons and technology, as well as to facilitate the execution of tactical manoeuvres, the ingraining of established combat drills was essential – if only to help commanders and soldiers under stress to overcome fear and concentrate on their tasks. The German recruits were particularly well trained at least until 1943. From brigade level downwards, battle procedures were sharpened and battle drills were instituted within battalions to inculcate the responsibilities of each member down to the rifleman. Tactical doctrine was widely revised, and the battle drills obliged rifle companies and platoons to organize all-round defence of their position, and to practise the manoeuvre of fire and movement in attack from the rifle section upwards.

New standards of physical fitness led to greater energy in fieldcraft, in alertness for observation and in strength to carry and use effectively the range of infantry weapons (further detailed in Chapter 5). Live rounds were introduced into certain field exercises and training officers were excused occasional casualties. The quality of training was raised by forming battle schools for leaders to develop expertise and initiative. A new range of training pamphlets, using cartoons and sketches as much as words to illustrate lessons were widely issued. Studies and evaluations were made about enemy equipment.

Accomplished by reports from front line units and other sources such as foreign publications coming from neutral sources, the Germans were able to collect technical data and build up a good library on the materials opposing them. The results of these researches were used as a basis for lectures and comments to student NCOs and officers in the training schools. Officers who could not adjust adequately to the new dynamics were replaced; the average age of commanding officers fell by 1943 from 40 to 30 years. German infantry expertise was rising in many environments: desert, street fighting, mountain, winter conditions, and after 1943, defensive warfare. Military historians often agree that, at low level, German privates were both disciplined and individualistic, properly trained, strongly motivated and well led. On the whole, they fought well even without close supervision; they could improvise in emergencies, generally continued fighting after losing officers and remained effectively organized right down to the last NCO.

However in the last two years of the war, training was rather low and the German Army was no longer as effective as it had once been. It took a very severe shaking once the unrealized power of the Allied air forces and artillery was let loose on it. Most of the selected highly experienced original soldiers of the early days of the war had long gone. Their places were increasingly filled by hastily trained and less motivated soldiers who – despite all the Nazi promises concerning 'wonder weapons' – were more and more sceptical of total victory because recruitment, armament and training were becoming poor, while the Allied pressure grew stronger.

German mountain units initially received the same basic training as regular infantrymen. A high standard of discipline and hardness was required. So, as with all recruits from all branches of service, training for Gebirgsjäger recruits was particularly hard. Trainees were put through their paces in parade marching, weapons drill, marksmanship in all kind of weapons, and the usual polishing and cleaning that accompanies all basic military training.

Specialized mountain training came afterwards. The main tasks of the Gebirgsjäger were combat in extreme weather conditions, winter warfare, and warfare in arctic and mountain terrains, so training was adapted in consequence. Officers were instructed to lead detachments at most times not larger than battalion size as this was realistically the largest size that could be deployed in such areas. Battalion officers had to be trained army mountaineering guides and each year pass tests. All officers and guides were exercised at map reading and familiar with the use of the altimeter. Good mountaineer officers were by experience able to judge the changing weather and quickly recognize mountain dangers.

As sound travels further in the mountains than across flat country, great emphasis was placed on movement without noise. Troops were trained to be most economical in their expenditure of ammunition. The trainees of course, received thorough instruction in map reading and compass marches, but also in igloo building, traversing icefields, crossing crevasses and cracks, rock climbing, abseiling, cross-country skiing, as well as marching at night. A great emphasis was placed on marching as not all formations were or could be motorized. When the regular infantryman's equipment was usually carried by the (motorized) divisional baggage train, the Gebirgsjäger's main form of transport was his own two feet and pack animals. Therefore the typical mountain trooper had to be a supremely fit individual, who carried a considerable amount of regular equipment, food, and ammunition as well as specific gear. With this heavy load on his back he was expected to march and fight, but also to be proficient at scaling, escalating, clambering and climbing mountains. Pack animals proved fairly efficient and were widely used for carrying supplies, collective material, disassembled artillery, and ammunitions. So many Jäger had to possess knowledge of caring and controlling these animals. The use of pack animals also meant that progress during an advance was much slower than a motorized unit and held many more dangers.

Men who had been born in mountain areas had learned some of the required skills such as skiing and climbing from a very early age, and it was these specialists who acted as mountain guides as well as leading assaults in high mountainous areas.

Whenever Gebirgsjäger were employed in their intended role hardships were commonplace. In Poland and Russia, they undertook endless and exhausting marches across immense plains swept by snow and wind in winter, and burnt by choking heat and dry dust in summer. In northern Norway, Finland and Lapland they experienced the bitter Arctic weather and the freezing conditions of the Caucasus heights in Southern Russia. In Yugoslavia, they encountered the numerous harsh and inhospitable Balkan ranges, and in France the formidable Alpine massif. In northern Italy they fought in the Alps and the Dolomites, as well as in the other ranges like the Appenine. In the Greek mainland and islands (notably in Crete) they faced the heat of the desolate and arid steep hills.

Gebirgsjäger, just like paratroopers and submarine crews, had to possess exceptional mental strength and physical energy. They had to be well trained with a high degree of stamina to cope with the hardships that they encountered and the abnormal circumstances of living, moving and fighting at high altitude in an extremely demanding environment. This required exceptionally fit men having a high sense of comradship and a strong team spirit.

German mountain troops were also involved as conventional infantry, and on many occasions they took part in ground operations on normal terrain, along with regular foot soldiers. When used as conventional light infantry their specialist skills and training were wasted – a similar situation to that which Fallschirmjäger found themselves in. The lack of heavy support artillery, armoured vehicles and fully motorized transport units within their divisional structure often left them at a disadvantage when employed in this conventional role.

Oath

After months of intensive training, mountain troopers had to swear an oath of allegiance. The oath – since the decree of August 1934 – was not sworn as a token of loyalty to the constitution of the Weimar Republic (which had not been abrogated after the seizure of power by the Nazis) and to the People and the Fatherland, but to the Führer Adolf Hitler personally. The oath to Hitler was thus illegal, but in Nazi Germany lawfullness, justice, and equity was what Hitler had decided. The oath was mandatory for military personnel both volunteer and conscripts, and compulsory for all officials and civil servants.

It took place during a kind of solemn Nazi ceremony. New recruits formed a square on the parade ground of their home regimental depot, and with one hand on the Reich's War Flag (although in some cases a sword or a gun barrel draped in the regimental colours) and with one hand raised solemnly proclaimed: *'Ich schwöre bei Gott diesen heiligen Eid dass ich dem Führer des Deutschen Reiches und Volkes Adolf Hitler, dem obersten Befehlshaber der Wehrmacht, unbedingten gehorsamheiten und als tapferer Soldat bereit sein will, jederzeit für diesen Eid mein Leben einzusetzen.'* ('I swear by God this sacred oath, that I will render unconditional obedience to Adolf Hitler, the Führer of the German Reich and people, Supreme Commander of the Armed Forces, and will be ready as a brave soldier to risk my life at any time for this oath.')

Refusal or reluctance to swear the oath was not tolerated and inevitably entailed dismissal, loss of job, and arrest. To military personnel accustomed to obey, and traditionaly with a strong feeling of honour, the oath was taken seriously, and had an enormous impact. Officers and men found themselves *unconditionally* honour-bound to obey Hitler, thus even when ordered to commit dishonourable unsoldiery actions. Indeed, such was the straitjacket in which Hitler's oath had bound his generals, officers and soldiers that – on the whole – few complaints and no serious obstructions were raised against those well-known large scale Nazi war crimes, exactions, atrocities and genocide.

Henceforth refusal to obey orders, desertion or rebellion was a crime committed against Hitler himself. *Fahnenflucht* or *uberlaufen* literally 'abandon the flag' or 'running away'; actually desertion was regarded in Nazi Germany as an offence against the Führer, the *Volksgemeinschaft* (national community) and the *Wehrkraftzersetzung* (a brutal law against subversion of the war effort). In April 1940, Hitler issued guidelines, which prescribed the death sentence as being the normal punishment. Estimations show that during the Second World War, about 35,000 soldiers of the German forces were accused of desertion, resulting in about 22,750 death sentences of which at least 15,000 (maybe more) were carried out. This amazingly high figure can be largely explained by the extreme measures imposed by the SS on German commanders and troops during the last year of the war. Indeed any soldier not wounded, picked up outside his unit area, was to be arbitrarily tried and shot.

The oath marked the continuation of Hitler's cult of personality, the increased politization and nazification of the armed forces, and a further step into *Gleichschaltung* – a series of decrees, laws and measures aiming to fundamentally restructure German society, army and culture along strict racist Nazi lines.

In the first third of the twentieth century, Germany was arguably the most technologically sophisticated and scientifically advanced nation in the world. Acclaimed since the eighteenth century as 'the land of poets, musicians, philosophers, and Nobel Prize recipients' it had also developed within the European traditions of Christianity and the enlightenment, with their respective emphases on love, art and reason. How could such a nation have produced the Third Reich, possibly the most murderous society in history?

The answer is not easy, and seems to lie in the racist ideology that formed the Nazi worldview. Also, military discipline greatly contributed to keeping soldiers obedient, but this was achieved only by profoundly perverting the nature and meaning of discipline and 'honour'. This corrupting process had an important impact on the troops' conduct and state of mind, and ultimately led to a widespread brutalization of combat units.

Harsh military discipline had a long tradition in Germany, stretching back to the days of corporal punishment, blind obedience, and draconian drills of Frederick the Great's Prussian army.

Just like organization and planning, strict discipline and rigorous obedience were the trademarks of the German military long before Hitler came to power. Nevertheless, it was obvious that under influence of Nazi racist ideology especially during the war, the theory and practice of martial law in the Wehrmacht underwent fundamental and crucial changes. These changes reflected and enhanced the overall transformation of the army's character, and were responsible not only for the troops' steadfastness on the battlefield, but also for their profound brutalization.

From the very beginning military discipline in the Third Reich's army was closely tied to the ideological tenets of the regime, notably ultranationalism, political intolerance, legalized criminality, the cult of war and violence, ruthlessness permissible by law, nihilism, xenophobia, anti-semitism, and extreme racism. These principles and beliefs held by the regime were imposed and became more or less accepted by the Wehrmacht as the normal rules of war. This resulted in unsoldiery actions, atrocities, mass murder and crimes against humanity in and outside the battlefields perpetrated not only by the SS but also by regular Wehrmacht soldiers.

Chapter Four

Uniforms & Regalia

German Uniforms

Generalities

Insignia and uniforms in one way or another have been used ever since men banded together to go to war. Insignia and uniforms help distinguish enemy, ally and friend, leader and subordinate, expert and novice, and set apart military and civilian. They denote ranks and station, they indicate a soldier's skills and trades, and also display service, arm, regiment and national group. Insignia and uniforms are totemic elements giving a visible authority and status, and differentiate membership of a special or privileged group. Insignia and uniforms boost morale, provide political inspiration, and encourage enlistment and commitment. Insignia and badges are often aesthetically pleasing, they often have a striking or attractive, even fascinating design.

Obviously comfortable and adequate clothing was (and still is) very important if a fighting man is to operate at maximum efficiency. The design of a modern uniform must take into consideration many points such as the service in which it is going to be used, the equipment complementary to it, camouflage, serviceability, the comfort of the wearer and other practical considerations. German Second World War infantrymen had to carry with them a great deal of personal equipment to make each of them a single functioning unit. Particularly, armoured vehicle personnel, paratroopers and mountain troops required uniforms and equipment which adequately answered to the specific conditions in which they operated.

Since the First World War (1914–1918), the colours of uniforms were intentionally designed so as to merge into smoky, muddy, bracken or forested backgrounds, therefore using all combinations and shades of greyish green, khaki, or brown for the best concealment. Since 1910, the German troops wore a *Feldgrau* uniform (field-grey actually greyish/green) replacing the 'Prussian dark blue' colour, which had been the traditional service dress colour of the Prussian and German Armies in the nineteenth century.

By the Second World War, uniforms had become almost totally functional, yet there was still much room for variety. The demands for camouflage were paramount and the expansion of operations led to new adaptations such as motley smocks, snow-white suits in winter, and sand-yellow/light brown dress in desert battlegrounds.

In 1936, one year after the reintroduction of military conscription in Germany, new uniforms were issued. The conformity and the quality of all regalia and uniforms were controlled by the Army Ordnance Office. All army personnel were provided with a *Waffenrock* (parade uniform) and a *Dienstanzug* (service uniform) which, with addition of field equipment, also served as a *Feldanzug* (field uniform). On the whole German Second World War uniforms were well designed and manufactured with a great degree of standardization, combining functionality, and a rather smart appearance.

German uniforms also underwent a number of changes made necessary by the increasing diversity of climate and terrain in which the troops fought, and by the variety of tactical requirements to which they were subjected. However, if troops entered combat zones with regulation dress, the ravages of fighting were hard on uniforms. After 1943, replacement supplies from behind the lines were not always forthcoming and soldiers tended to take what was available and make do. Front-line soldiers in the last phase of the war therefore often wore odd mixtures of original issue items from other friendly troops and occasionally fallen foes and even articles that were stolen or borrowed on the spot. Indeed the unexpected prolongation of the war and the effective blockade brought upon Germany, resulted in shortage of raw materials, and therefore a need for simplification, and the use of poorer quality cloth. Whereas the enlisted man's wool service dress countained 20 per cent rayon mixed with it in 1939, the uniforms made after 1943 onward had 50 per cent or even less wool content mixed with low grade recycled material. The Germans also made good use of captured stocks of clothing and equipment obtained from the armies of the countries they occupied. Austrian army uniforms were re-cut, dyed and modified, and the same occured with uniforms and equipment from Norway, the Netherlands, Poland, France, and later Italy. Huge stocks of captured military supplies were converted to conform as closely as possible to German regulations, and issued to regular troops, auxiliary forces and police units. So old and discarded Reichswehr uniforms, and equipment as well as foreign captured items were worn and used during the war until stocks were out.

As the war went on and on, it took its toll on equipment and supplies of raw materials, and quality declined everywhere. By 1944–45, all attempts to maintain top quality had gone, the only goal was to meet the needs of the military machine with whatever was available in the best and cheapest way possible.

Basic Uniforms

Uniform, weapons and equipment used by the mountain troops were on the whole the same as those used by the regular German light infantry. However special items were issued to meet the extreme conditions in which mountain troopers operated. The basic mountain uniform followed the standard Army pattern including a mouse-grey shirt, a four-pocketed tunic, and a matching pair of trousers. The main differences between regular Heer and mountain troops' uniforms were:

The variety of trousers, pants, knickerbockers, ski-trousers as well as knee-length fairly wide-legged Alpine trousers often worn with long thick woollen puttees or stockings; the addition of various camouflaged smocks, warm anoraks, wind jackets and baggy overgarments; distinctive headgear – notably the special peaked mountain cap; heavy footwear, notably strong climbing shoes with studded soles often replacing the typical Heer jackboots.

Fatigue

A basic wartime German uniform was the so-called *Drillichanzug* (fatigue suit). This was a white/light-grey work suit made of unbleached denim material. It consisted of a shapeless buttoned jacket with two patch pockets and a turn down collar; the trousers, made in the same material, had a simple cut with two side pockets. The fatigue suit was easily washable and used extensively for menial tasks, work, instruction, training manoeuvres, weapon cleaning and motor vehicle maintenance. As it was rather light it could also be used as alternative summer dress.

Field uniform

For economic reasons the German Army field uniform was designed to perform the purposes of field and service uniform and for walking out. In wartime, the field uniform was worn in combat and on all occasions except those that call for a fatigue or work uniform. As the war progressed the quality of the field uniform tended to decrease, particularly for low ranks. The field uniform included the following components some of which underwent changes during the war: headgear (steel helmet, and various caps); underwear; shirt; tunic with four pockets; trousers held up with suspenders or a waist belt; various footwear (jackboots or heavy duty boots or shoes with protective gaiters or leggings); as well as all the necessary fighting equipment and accoutrements described in Chapter 6.

The field uniform was *Feldgrau* (grey-green) in colour, but there were some variations in its actual shade depending on deterioration due to wear-and-tear, age, and amount of cleaning.

The depicted Hauptmann (Captain) wears the officer's service dress with peaked cap; field grey tunic with dark green collar; riding breeches; and polished riding boots.

Mountain officers wore a uniform similar to the regular infantry but with the Edelweiss badge sewn on the right sleeve.

The German basic uniform in 1940 included a cap, a shirt, a tunic, a pair of trousers and jackboots.

The private wears the M35 steel helmet; the field grey woollen tunic with green piping colour on the collar patches, and the shoulder straps, and a stone grey pair of trousers tucked into marching jackboots. On the black leather waistbelt he carries triple pocket ammunition leather pouches. He is armed with a Mauser 7.92 mm Kar 98K carbine.

Drillichanzug (fatigue).

This mountain trooper NCO wears the regular army uniform including a *Bergmütze* (mountain cap), and a simplified lightweight field-grey tunic with unpleated pockets, and dark green collar. The field-grey mountain trousers (called Hose) were held up by a belt or braces. They were hard wearing, high waisted, and fairly baggy. They had a reinforced seat and crotch and had the legs tapered to tuck into canvas gaiters, and black leather mountain shoes. The man is armed with a *Maschinenpistole 40* (sub-machine gun) and magazine pouches clipped on his waistbelt.

Left: The *Feldbluse* (field/service tunic) model 1936 had four pockets, a turned-back collar with rank and arm insignia indicated on patches on the revers. The tunic colour was *Feldgrau* (field grey-green), and around the waist it had hooks and metal supports to which the waistbelt fitted. The front of the tunic was secured by five or six grey painted buttons.

Right: Tunic pattern 1943. As the war lengthened, Germany's resources were stretched and economies led to uniform changes. The tunic pattern 1943 was simplified, and made of inferior material, giving uniforms a shoddy appearance and poor thermal insulation.

Originally German army shirts were white, and after 1940 for camouflage purposes they were field or mouse grey. Shirts came in several variants, short or long with long tails reaching down to mid-thigh length, with or without long sleeves, with or without breast pockets, with or without shoulder straps. Some were pullover type, others fully open at the front and fitted with buttons. Some were thick and warm and made of knitted wool-like material, others were light and made of cotton drill.

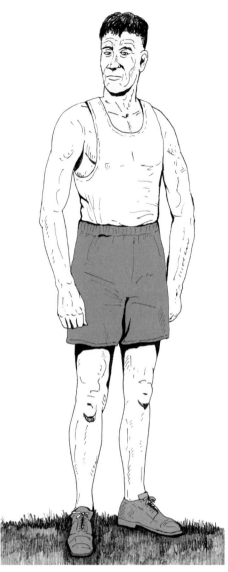

Sport played an important role in the training of all German soldiers, so each man was issued a sport kit comprising a white singlet, black shorts with elasticated waist, and low, laced soft leather sport shoes generally worn without socks. For water sport each man was issued a short swimming trunk.

The pressure of economics in war conditions caused the introduction in September 1944 of a new simplified uniform. The model 44 was quite similar to the British battledress uniform, including a cheap short blouse with only two unpleated chest pockets, and trousers of inferior quality.

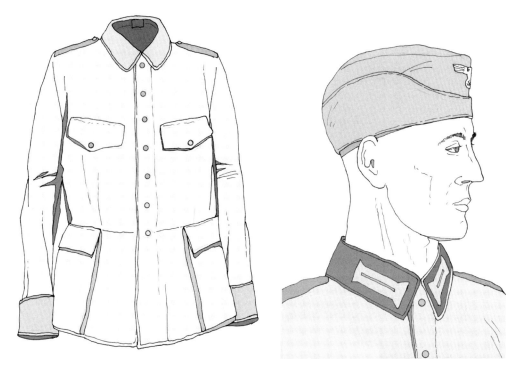

Left: Dutch tunic. This captured Dutch army tunic was adapted to German regulation with the addition of a dark grey collar and two large pockets.
Right: Captured Czech *Feldmütze* (service forage peakless hat).

Parade dress

For review, muster, commemorations, ceremonial occasions, and formal duties, German soldiers were issued a *Waffenrock* (parade dress). Introduced in June 1935, this suit was composed of trousers and tunic made in superior *Feldgrau* greyish/green material. The trousers, in matching shade, were straight or a riding style with a thin piping *Waffenfarbe* (colour of service) on the outer leg seams. The tunic was pocketless, single breasted, closed up to the neck by eight metal buttons; it had turned-up Swedish-style cuffs faced with dark bottle green material, shoulder straps and collar bearing *Waffenfarbe* (colour of service), piping and *Litzen* (braid) patches. With the parade uniform the enlisted soldier wore a peaked hat or the M35 steel helmet, marching boots, the standard service belt often carrying ammunition pouches and bayonet. Occasionally the men marched with full field equipment including rucksack.

On parade the men carrying an Army standard or flag wore a sash composed of a wide leather-backed, heavy gauge silver braid with silk embroidery in the colour of the unit's *Waffenfarbe*; the sash, worn over the left shoulder across the body, included a leather cup to hold the base of the flag pole. Army standard or flag bearers also wore a regimental *Ringkragen* (gorget). Originally the gorget was part of a medieval armour, a plate worn to protect the throat. It developed into an ornamental crescent-shaped metal device, engraved or embossed with coat-of-arms etc. Neglected for about a century, the gorget re-appeared in Germany in the 1930s, when it was worn by flag-bearers and military policemen. It consisted of a bronze half-moon-shaped shield positioned under the collar on the breast by a metal chain; the item was decorated with Nazi regalia including bosses, oakleaves, *Hoheitszeichen* and swastika. Flag-bearers were also distinguished by a special badge worn on the right upper-arm carrying crossed flags in their regimental colours, the Wehrmacht eagle/swastika and an oak leaf. Parade marching required training as the troops held the rifle on the left shoulder and walked the typical, physically demanding *Paradeschritt* (German 'goose-step'), marching with legs lifted and straight.

Officers' parade dress was quite similar, but generally of better quality and more elegant than lower ranks. With it officers, army officials and generals wore either the

This Hauptmann (Captain) wears the regular field-grey *Waffenrock* (parade dress). The tunic, collar and cuffs were piped in light green, and aiguillettes – braid ornament loops hung from the shoulder. The mountain cap or the steel helmet were common wear on parade.

Parade tunic (*Waffenrock*).

M35 steel helmet or the *Schirmmütze* (a cap with stiff black peak), riding trousers and high leather riding boots with attached spurs. In addition musicians, senior officers and officers wore an *Achselband* (aiguillete – ornate plaited shoulder cord) attached below the right shoulder strap and looped over the right breast to the second button of the tunic. Re-introduced in June 1935, aiguilletes were more or less decorated and elaborated according to rank, seniority, specialisation and regimental tradition.

Another German ceremonial item was the *Portépée*, an adorned knot or ball tied around the hilt of the officer's ceremonial sword or dagger. A similar decoration used on NCOs' bayonets was the *Troddel* (side-arm tassel). Regulations for the solely decorative Aiguilletes, *Portépées* and *Troddeln* patterns and weaves were complex with specific coloured strap, slide, stem, crown and tassel indicating formation, seniority, rank and even historical regimental links. When the Second World War began, the parade dress was no longer issued, and only worn during the war on special occasions such as official ceremonies, burials or weddings by those who still had the pre-war issue. The Aiguilletes, *Portépées* and *Troddeln* had no function other than that of pure decoration, and were no longer issued after April 1943.

This was the dress uniform, which in turn was divided into *grossen* (ceremonial) and *kleine* (ordinary or minor occasions) *Gesellschaftanzug*. Long trousers and high black shoes were always worn with this type of uniform. It included service cap, service coat, long piped trousers, high black shoes, and black belt with sword (for senior non-commissioned officers) or decorative bayonet (for junior non-commissioned officers and men). Decorations and awards were of course proudly displayed.

Panzer uniform

The *Panzerwaffe* (armoured force) was officially created in 1935, and was rapidly transformed from an experimental and largely clandestine department into an important fighting branch of the German army with divisional formations. Armoured troops (including armoured reconnaissance cars' crews) were newcomers without tradition in the German army and a special uniform, *Sonderbekleidung der Deutschen Panzertruppen* (special uniform for the German armoured force) was designed for them in November 1934. The German special tank uniform was black. It consisted of a jacket and trousers worn with a grey shirt and black tie. The Panzer *Feldjacke* was a short hip-length, double-breasted, tight-fitting jacket, without external pockets and no external features, which would snag inside an armoured vehicle. It had a deep fall collar and broad lapels

The black Panzer uniform included a thick protection beret (until 1940), a short double-breasted tunic, matching trousers, and jackboots.

The collar lapels displayed the armoured badge decorated with a Death's Head with crossed bones.

decorated with collar piping and the emblem of the Panzerwaffe: a parallelogram cloth badge with a small metallic-silver Death's Head with crossed bones quite similar to that of the SS.

The *Feldhose* (trousers) were the same for all ranks: they were black, full length and slightly baggy. They were fastened around the ankle and usually tucked into the *Marschstiefel* (marching jackboots) giving a deep 'pull-down' effect. After 1941 the army boots were replaced with *Schnürschue* (ankle-length laced shoes) with short *Gamaschen* (canvas gaiters).

Headgear originally consisted of a thick crash beret called *Schutzmütze* (protection cap). The roundish peakless Panzer beret was black, padded with rubber lining, and fitted with ventilation holes. Its front was decorated with the inevitable eagle/swastika and a cockade. After 1940 the *Schutzmütze* proved rather impractical during combat, and was replaced with various army headgear including peaked and peakless caps as well as the standard army steel helmet.

The *Sonderbekleidung* was worn by crews of combat armoured vehicles (aka tanks). As for the crews of self-propelled guns they were artillerymen, but wore the same uniform except for the colour that was grey or green.

Some mountain divisions included a tank or a self-propelled anti-tank formation. The men operating those vehicles wore the black or grey Panzer suit described above, but with the distinctive Edelweiss mountain emblem.

Of all the uniforms issued to the mountain troops, the black armoured vehicle dress was by far the least common. Actually, only one mountain division, namely the 7th SS Freiwilligen Gebirgs Division Prinz Eugen had an armoured unit. It was equipped with captured French tanks, mainly Renault R7.

Summer Uniforms

In summer on the southern Russian front, and in Southern Europe and Mediterranean theatres, mountain troopers were issued tropical uniforms and equipment similar to those designed for the German Africa Corps. This *Tropenbekleidung* (summer or tropical clothing) intended for troops operating in desert conditions in North Africa was light brown, sand-yellowish or pale olive green in colour. It featured several garments like shorts made of denim-type material, baggy light trousers, light shirts – some sleeveless – lightweight denim summer tunic often mixed with other pieces of uniform. Soldiers could also simply resort to wearing shirtsleeve order. In spite of cotton shortages, the summer tunic, coat and trousers continued to be of good quality cotton twill. Since late 1942, however, the four pleated pockets of the tunic were simplified and modified in the same fashion as those of the normal field uniform coat. The summer dress originally included a *Tropenhelm* (tropical helmet) made of cork covered with olive green cotton drill. Proving highly impractical, it was soon replaced with the same basic headgear worn with the regular uniform, but caps and hats were made of light canvas instead of thick warm wool. The light peaked cap was particularly popular as it protected the eyes from the sun.

This Oberfeldwebel (NCO) wears the light canvas version of the *Bergmütze* known as M43 field cap; a lightweight green denim summer tunic; a pair of pale olive denim shorts; and light grey socks rolled down over the top of the mountain shoes. He is armed with a P38 pistol in a leather holster fixed on his waistbelt.

The tropical uniform designed for the Afrikakorps was widely worn by mountain troopers in Southern Europe in the summertime. It was sand-yellow/ligh brown in colour, and included a field cap, a light field blouse, light baggy trousers, and mountain boots and gaiters.

Accoutrements, notably belts and straps were made from olive-green light webbing material instead of leather. For camouflage purpose, the standard steel helmet, the cylindrical gasmask container, the typical black leather ammunition pouches for rifles, carbines, and MPi sub-machine guns, and all other pieces of equipment were usually painted in pale green/yellow or light olive-brown.

The *Mantel* (overcoat) was a standard pattern throughout the German Army. Issued and worn by all ranks, it was basically a very long double-breasted garnment reaching to the wearer's calf. Mostly field-grey in colour with a dark blue/green collar, it was slightly waisted and had rows of grey metal buttons (gilded for generals), deep turn-back cuffs and usually two large side-slash pockets. There were several variants, notably thicker lined versions, made of sheepskins and furs especially intended and issued for sentry duty in the field.

A variant was the rubberized *Schutzmantel* (protective overcoat) issued to motorcyclists. This was loose fitting, waterproof, and the tail of the garment could be gathered in around the wearer's legs and buttoned in position for easier and safer movement when riding a bike. After 1943, for reasons of economy, modified versions of the greatcoat made from inferior quality material were introduced and issued to the troops.

Officers and generals were entitled to purchase their own greatcoats made from fine grain quality leather for parade, service and field service. For informal occasions and service, senior officers were also issued with a long sleeveless grey cloak with a dark blue-green collar. The cloak reached down to the wearer's calf, and had five buttons, and two side pocket openings. There was a variant made of rubber for wear on rainy days and bad weather.

Mantel.

Mantel variants.

Sheep skin *Mantel*.

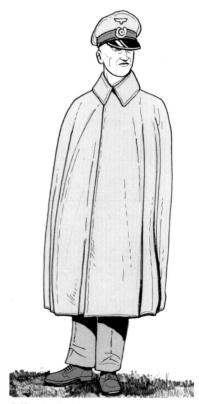

Officer's cloak.

Winter Suits

Prior to the winter of 1941–42, the German Army made little provision for winter warfare. Mountain troops were the best equipped to fight under conditions of extreme cold and snow, while the remainder of the Army received special clothing only for special missions and duties. Sentries were the only soldiers, besides drivers and motorcyclists, who were provided with specially designed warm clothing. During the first winter

Two-piece 1943 model reversible winter suit with hood, shown with the camouflaged side.

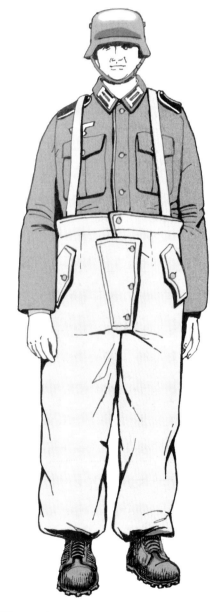

Winter suit trousers.

on the Russian front (1941–42) German soldiers adopted every kind of improvisation in order to survive in the extreme cold, with fur, leather, cloth, wool and even straw before a suitable regular winter combat suit was introduced. The *Winterwaffenrock* (winter suit) was first issued on the Russian front in winter 1942–43 as a result of the bitter experience of the previous winter. Designed specifically to resist the severe sub-zero weather conditions encountered on the Eastern front, smocks and overtrousers were made of two thick layers of windproof and waterproof cloth with a woollen lining. The double-breasted smock was fitted with a detachable hood. The winter suit was generally worn over the field service uniform; the ammunition pouches, holsters and other items were carried on the normal belt over it; the suit had patch pockets in the smock and side pockets on the trousers. The winter suit was constantly improved, notably with the layers of windproof cloth and interliners, and thus existed in several variants, some reversible – all white on one side and mottled green/brown camouflage on the other. Some fortunate units were issued with thick white quilted winter parkas or warm sheepskin

Schneeanzug, winter 'snow suit' with hood worn under the M35 steel helmet, quilted parka, overtrousers, and straw-boots.

coats, fur-lined greatcoats with a fur collar but these luxuries were often in short supply and reserved for officers. On the Russian front where conditions were particularly

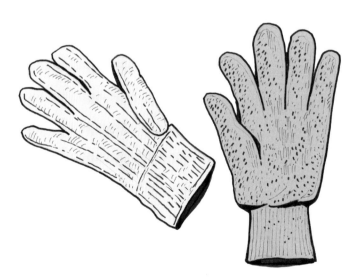
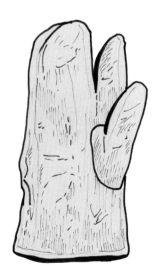

Gloves and mittens.

awful, soldiers in need wore a mixture of regular Army issues and captured Russian military or civilian clothes or sheepskins, fur coats, Russian felt boots, and strawboot covers. Various kinds of woollen scarves, as well as gloves, padded mittens and gauntlets, completed the winter suit, some mittens had a loose forefinger to enable pulling the trigger of a firearm. For cleaning and repair purposes as well as replacement with fresh stocks, winter cloths were collected from the troops in spring and returned to the front for redistribution during the following autumn.

Anoraks & Camouflaged Dress

Mountain troops were the best equipped to fight under conditions of extreme cold and snow. The remainder of the Army received special clothing only for exceptional missions and duties. Sentries, drivers and motorcyclists were the only soldiers who received specially designed warm clothing like surcoats, thick greatcoats and felt overboots, or, if the latter were lacking, straw overboots.

The field uniforms, clothing and equipment intended for mountain warfare had to offer comfort and freedom of movement for mobility and combat. Combat dresses and field uniforms were always rather roomy, baggy and loose fitting allowing an insulating layer of air as protection against cold and wind, and also as a means of body ventilation avoiding the accumulation of sweat and dampness caused by efforts and physical exertion.

Mountain troops were issued with a reversible heavy padded double-breasted winter suit with hood attached. Several types of *Windblusen* (wind and waterproof anoraks) were issued. Intended for wear over the service tunic, some were front buttoned, while others were pull-on jackets with attached hood, chest pockets, waist belt, bottom drawstring, elasticated wrist and reinforced shoulder and elbows.

A specific mountain troop cold weather item was the *Windjacke*, a sage green waterproof wind jacket reaching to the thighs, with adjustable cuffs, double breasted and loose fitting, with two skirt pockets. A warm reversible camouflage smock was also issued which had a white lining and a hood; it was worn over the service tunic and had a white outside when operating in winter or above the snow line, and a green/brown camouflage side when operating in forested areas.

Anoraks and smocks were issued in three weights. The most common was the

Windjacke.

The standard-issue mountain troop *Windjacke* (wind jacket) as the name implies was windproof. It was double-breasted with adjustable cuffs, was grey/green, had a large collar, and shoulder straps. It was worn over the regular field tunic.

This MG 34 machine-gunner wears the popular *Bergmütze*; a reversible pull-over grey mountain anorak with three breast pockets (which was reversible – grey on one side and snow white on the other) and attached hood; field grey trousers; puttees and mountain shoes. On his belt he carries a 9 mm pistol in its holster, and a machine-gun maintenance pouch containing stripping tools, cleaning kit, and other gear for the MG34 machine-gun.

medium weight, in which the material consisted of two layers of windproof cloth with a rayon-wool interliner. The windproof cloth had the same water-repellent feature as the latest mountain parka. Since the complete uniform contained only 9 per cent wool, the clothing was rather heavy for its warmth, and therefore not as efficient as the designers had planned. The basic moutain field uniform originally had a white and a field-grey side, but by 1943 the need for better camouflage had become so apparent that a mottled camouflaged design was substituted for field-grey. After a number of improvisations, two designs of mottle were used, one was that of the regular shelter/cape/poncho, and the other was that of the Army camouflage jacket.

The depicted ski-trooper is quite well camouflaged for operating in snowy environment. He wears the regular *Bergmütze* with a loose white snow cover; snow goggles with tinted glasses; a reversible grey-to-white pullover anorak with attached hood and three breastpockets and thick white overtrousers. Anorak and trousers were donned over the regular grey mountain uniform. The man's hands are protected with thick white padded woollen mittens, featuring a trigger finger allowing him to fire his rifle without removing his gloves. His leather belt and the ammunition pouches for the rifle are smeared with whitewash for camouflage purposes.

The so-called *Windbluse* pull-over windproof anorak was grey on one side and white on the other.

Anoraks, parkas, and jackets were supplied with matching overtrousers, which were fairly baggy, tapered at the bottom to allow them to be tucked into the gaiters. Special trousers were issued for skiing, they too were rather baggy, often made of the usual field-grey wool-rayon cloth, and fitted with tapes at the ankles. Trousers and overpants were usually issued with special mountain suspenders. This clothing went together with warm pull-over shirts, knitted woollen sweaters, jerseys, turtleneck woollen pullovers, and gloves for added warmth.

Snipers as well as observers and sentries posted in advanced positions were usually issued complete camouflaged suits (often improvised) including felt face masks, aka balaclavas protecting head, face and neck from wind and cold.

Camouflaged tunics

Camouflage uniforms were not introduced into the army until 1942. Before that time, the only units issued with expensive (and at first experimental) camouflage uniforms were the élite paratroopers, the infantry field divisions of the Luftwaffe, the Herman Göring Regiment (later Division), and the Waffen SS – as discussed in Part 7.

The *Tarnjacke* (camouflaged tunic) was based on the typical Waffen SS garment. It existed in several variants, some reversible with one side white and the other combining various motley tans such as brown, green, red, pink, yellow, grey and black printed in irregular patterns. In late 1943, stocks of repellent camouflage clothes captured from the Italian army were converted to make trousers and jackets.

Regular Army soldiers were issued a *Körperschürze* (body apron) made from a

Tarnjacke.

Körperschürze (body apron).

Tarnkappe or *Zeltbahn* (camouflaged poncho).

simple large piece of cotton. The apron, pulled over the service/field uniform, was about knee-length, it had a V-shaped collarless neck opening and tapes, which could be tied under the arms. It was large enought so equipment could fit under or over it. The garb was reversible, on one side it had camouflage coloured brown/green motley patterns for use in spring and summer and on the other side plain white for winter use in snow.

Each German soldier was issued a triangular *Tarnkappe* (camouflaged cape) which could be used as a poncho for cold and rain, and as a tent quarter. This universally popular item is further described in Chapter 6 in the section on equipment.

During the battle of Normandy in summer 1944, some troops experimented with improvised string vests permitting camouflage for the body with fresh cut foliage, grass and brushwood. Snipers were often issued with complete camouflage suits (using German and Italian mottled fabrics), including face masks.

Special dress for motorcyclists and drivers

Motorcyclists were issued with a supplementary raincoat; a pair of goggles; a pair of thick and heavy gauntlets; and, in winter, an extra sweater, wool oversocks, and a special overcoat. The gauntlets were of overcoat cloth with a trigger finger, and may have had leather palms. The footless oversocks came up high on the leg. The raincoat was a special, long, rubber coat. It could be buttoned in a variety of ways to improve protection and to facilitate operation of the motorcycle. This rubberized overcoat was also issued to drivers of light vehicles. In winter, a surcoat was provided – a heavy wool garment cut like the overcoat, but sufficiently large to be worn over all clothing including the overcoat. Some surcoats had attached wool hoods. Drivers of all types of vehicles receive motorcyclists' gauntlets, and for cold weather the thick surcoat. Drivers of horse transport also received felt over-boots with wooden soles.

Footwear

The privates' trousers were tucked into three-quarter length black strong leather *Marschstiefel* (boots or jackboots) with hob nails, hoof irons, toe plates and studded soles. The boot's finish was pebbled or 'jacked' – a process which involved the use of wax and tar to make a hard surface. Officers and generals usually wore elegant smooth polished high leather riding boots with adjustable straps to the top and sometimes with attached spurs for parade. The traditional footgear of German soldiers for centuries, the jackboots, however, required an inordinate amount of leather and caused unnecessary wear on the heel caused by marching. The jack boots therefore received much adverse criticism in the German military press. Besides, leather became a precious commodity for industrial use. By 1941 the use of jackboots was limited to infantry, engineers and motorcyclists. From late 1943, material shortages forced a radical change and the issue of jackboots was finally suspended, although existing stocks were used up. Henceforth, the traditional marching boots were replaced with black lace-up ankle shoes worn with old-fashioned puttees, canvas or leather leggings, anklets or gaiters fastened with

German Second World War jackboot.

Insulated leather felt boots.

Shoes and gaiters.

Schnürschuhe (black lace-up ankle shoes) were issued. They featured a stout double sole reinforced with iron studs and iron cleats around the edge, giving a good support to the ankle and enhancing the mountain infantrymen's mobility. These shoes were usually worn with old-fashioned wool puttees, canvas or leather leggings, anklets or gaiters fastened by buckles.

buckles. On all parades and on field service, regulation footwear was obligatory. Off duty any form of black boot was allowable, both for commissioned and other ranks, but authorities frowned upon civilian items.

For mountain troops, *Bergschuhe* (climbing boots) with cleats on the soles were issued instead of Army jackboots. These boots with their heavily studded soles were often worn with grey-green puttees (aka *leggings* in American). Puttees were long woollen strips (about 30 in) wound spirally around the leg from ankle to knee for protection and support. Footgear was usually large enough to permit the toes to move freely. In addition to inner soles, soldiers wore one or two pairs of thick woollen socks, which were frequently changed. In extreme low temperature, the feet are especially susceptible to frostbite, and eventually a pair of foot-wrapping cloth, straw or paper soles were worn for extra warmth.

Greyish brown canvas or leather overshoes attached with leather straps were also worn. Extending above the shoes they protected a part of the foot, the ankle and the lower leg. Especially for skiing, leather winter boots were developed with various binding systems allowing the sole of the shoe to lock on the ski using a clipping indentation around the heel, a spring, and leather straps.

Headgear

Steel helmet M35

Gebirgstruppen wore the standard German Army headgear including the M35 steel helmet. The steel helmet issued in 1935, called *Stahlhelm M35*, with its distinctive 'coal scuttle' shape was one of the most characteristic items of equipment associated with the Second World War German soldier. The M35 was based on the 1915 *Stahlhelm* (steel helmet) model. Very well designed, it was stamped in one piece from a sheet of nickel-chromium steel. The helmet offered good protection against small calibre projectiles, shell splinters and flying debris to skull, face, ears and neck. It existed in several variants and sizes and featured two small ventilation holes. It was held on the head with a padded flexible leather lining with seven adjustable flaps mounted on a leather frame forming a kind of cushion, and a black leather adjustable chin strap. The *Stahlhelm* carried small decorations, which varied according to unit organization. It had small identification or insignia decals affixed to one or both sides. For the German light infantry, the right side bore a small tri-coloured shield with black, white, and red stripes – the traditional national colours of the German Empire. The left side of the helmet displayed a Wehrmacht decal insignia with an eagle holding a swastika. As the war went on, the decals were no longer applied for camouflage purposes. It was initially painted matt grey, but conditions meant that it was painted different shades, according to service and camouflage demands. To break up the sharp outline and to reduce reflection, the helmet could be wrapped with a sacking cover or a camouflaged cloth. In winter, the item was washed in white paint or garnished with unshaped pieces of white cloth held in place by canvas or leather straps. In spring the white paint was scrubbed off and the item was furnished with elasticated bands (cut from rubber tyre inner tubes), chicken wire mesh of woven string net, canvas or leather straps intended to hold camouflaging material such as fresh cut twigs, grass, foliage and brushwood.

M35 steel helmet.

Headgear camouflage was often improvised, since the Army did not provide a standard camouflage helmet cover until the issue of the camouflage jacket. But a very practical elastic band to fasten camouflage materials to the helmet was furnished to all troops. Camouflage clothing was usually organizational, and was issued for example to snipers, personnel of outposts, and sentinels.

Schirmmütze

Officers, NCOs and administrative personnel wore a *Schirmmütze*, a stiff wool or canvas service peaked cap. In various quality cloth and finish, this was worn with service dress, with parade dress and walking out uniform. The cap had a field-grey top, a dark blue-green material capband and a patent black shiny peak. Its high front included a chinstrap carrying *Waffenfarbe* pipings, the *Reichkokarde* hemmed with oak leaves around the coat of arms, and crowned by the eagle/swastika emblem.

There was also the widely worn *Offizierfeldmütze alterer Art* (officers' cap old model) which was a peaked cap rather similar to the *Schirmmütze* but smaller in outline and unstiffened.

Left: *Offizierfeldmütze alterer Art* – Officer peaked cap old pattern (soft).
Right: Officer peaked cap stiffened.

Feldmütze

All ranks from private to general wore a very popular *Feldmütze* (service forage cap). This was a garrison peakless cap made of grey material, designed so that it could also be worn under the steel helmet. It existed in various styles, finish and qualities, some were designed to allow the sides to be pulled down and buttoned around the wearer's ears. Sewn on the front of the cap was the national eagle insignia as on the tunic and

Left: Model 1938 *Feldmütze*; Right: Model 1942 *Feldmütze*.

the *Reichskokarde* (without oakleaves for low ranks) beneath an inverted chevron of *Waffenfarbe* arm of service piping; the national tricolour cocarde was surrounded by a wreath of oakleaves when worn by senior officers and generals.

Bergmütze

The *Bergmütze* (mountain hat) was the specific visored cap issued to mountain troops. Based on the First World War Austrian mountain model, it was cut from thick grey wool, and had side flaps which could be folded down to cover the ears. These flaps buttoned under the wearer's chin. Insignia consisted of an eagle/swastika badge above a national colour cockade, and a metal-stemmed Edelweiss worn on the left side. When operating in snow, the *Bergmütze* could be enveloped in a camouflage white cover. For senior officers the *Bergmütze* had gilt piping to the crown and gilt buttons fastening the side flaps. The *Bergmütze* was so popular that it became a general issue for all branches of the Wehrmacht in 1943, known as *Einheitsfeldmütze*.

Bergmütze (mountain cap).

Left: White cover for snow camouflage;
Right: Brown/green camo cover for forested terrain.

Einheitsfeldmütze

In June 1943, a new peaked field cap called *Einheitsfeldmütze* was introduced. It was based closely on the style of peaked cap worn by mountain troops and Afrika Korps soldiers. It was very convenient and popular, subsequently it became the most widely worn type of headgear on active service. It was made from light canvas for warm climates and from thick wool for cold weather. The warm version was a copy of the *Bergmütze* with side flaps which could be folded down and buttoned under the chin in cold weather, however, the protuding *Einheitsfeldmütze*'s semi-stiff visor was a little longer than the mountain cap's, giving more shade to the eyes. The national emblem eagle/swastika insignia and the rosette in

Camouflaged *Einheitsfeldmütze*.

national colours were displayed on the front. There were also a number of variants, notably a brown/green camouflaged peaked cap made of strong cotton fabric.

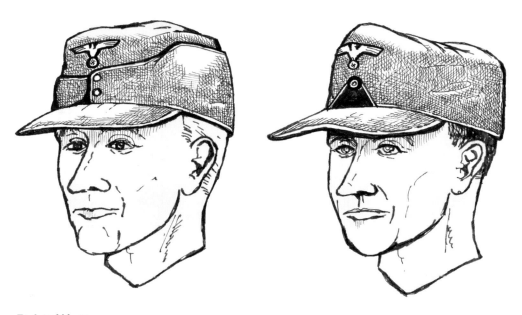

Einheitsfeldmütze.

Winter headgear

During the winter season, some German troops serving in the Eastern front or operating in the mountains were issued with Russian-styled *Pelzmützen* (fur covered caps) with ear, neck and front flaps faced with field grey cloth and rabbit-fur which could be tied down under the wearer's neck and chin. There was also a close fitting reversible hood protecting neck and shoulders; both toque and hood were part of the winter suit and were for wear under the M35 helmet. Other forms of cold conditions headdress included a wide range of improvisations and unofficial combinations of toque, cowls, wrap-around woollen scarves, woollen knitted bonnets, sheep fur caps, fur covered berets, *Kopschützer* (balaclava), close-fitting and brimless caps, Russian pingos (cowls), civilian mufflers and scarves were used.

Fur hat (*Pelzmütze*).

Left: The woollen knitted balaclava could be worn under a steel helmet or a *Bergmütze* (mountain cap); Right: Fur covered hat.

Regalia

The term *regalia* come from the Latin neuter plural of *regalis* ('of a king'), from *rex* ('king'). Originally regalia are thus the emblems or insignia of royalty, especially the ceremonial cloak, crown, orb, sceptre, and other ornaments used at a coronation. The term has been borrowed and came to be used by church, civic, military, politic, and Masonic fraternities. In the military context, regalia include strong symbols immediately comprehensible and impressive to all. These distinctive military tokens include ornaments and insignia (badge, cuff band, emblem, clasp, clip, pin, button, brooch, colour of service, piping, etc…) which are carried, worn, sewn or attached to a uniform as an official indication of nationality, status, rank and authority, speciality, qualification, branch of service, achievement, etc. Military insignia were and still are intended to establish clear differentiation between ranks and types of service, and at the same time to encourage individual combat efficiency and proficiency in military arts. Direct appeal was/is made to vanity, and to the human tendency to brag, boast, and show off military prowess as expressed in terms of insignia and decorations. Many Second World War insignia were based on traditional and historical German military regalia, with the addition of several specific Nazi features.

Hoheitszeichen

The most important insignia, worn on the German standard service uniform, was the Nazi emblem, which became the official national emblem, called *Hoheitszeichen*. Introduced in the German army in mid-1934, the woven or embroidered *Hoheitszeichen* (aka breast eagle) was worn over the right breast pocket by all ranks of the German Army (but not on camouflage dress). In a smaller metal version it decorated all army cloth-front headdress. The *Hoheitszeichen* was a styled eagle with outstreched wings (traditional German imperial emblem) clutching in its claws a wreath of oak leaves containing a swastika (Nazi party's hooked cross). Oak leaves – often combined with acorns in a wreath or a garland – were often used in Nazi regalia being linked with the laurel crown of Ancient Romans. They were powerful Nordic and Celtic symbols of life, and also represented strength, stability and nobility, as well as power, authority and victory.

The swastika (hooked cross or *Hakenkreuz* in German) was and still is the symbol the most readily associated with the Nazis. However, by no means did they create it. The swastika, widely used in Asian religions – notably Buddhism – was an adapted Greek cross with four arms of equal length extended at right or left angles. It originally symbolized the movement of the sun and the word swastika would mean good luck in Sanskrit, which was hardly what it came to represent under the Nazi régime. The Nazi swastika was often represented standing on one point to give the dynamic impression of an advancing movement.

The eagle, symbolizing prestige and strength, was a widely used token of heraldry used for example by the Egyptians, the Romans, the Caroligian empire, the medieval Holy Roman Germanic Reich, the United States of America and by the French emperor Napoleon Bonaparte. To the German people, it referred to the medieval Reich (Holy German Empire that existed from 962 to 1802), and to Hitler's followers it meant the recovery of the German national pride and greatness by way of Nazism.

The *Hoheitszeichen* existed in many styles and variations in design and colouring, in cloth or metal form, in combination with oakleaves, crown or wreath, and the eagle with overspreading or closed wings.

Various forms of Swastika.

Hoheitszeichen
Top: textile;
Bottom: metal.

Flag and songs

The German Second World War mountain troops' flag was a square piece of woven silk measuring about 126 × 126 cm attached to a black polished wooden pole surmounted by an aluminium point featuring an eagle and a swastika. The flag was bordered with a thin silver fringe. The cloth was dark green, and ornamented with four small black swastikas in the corners. A large 'iron cross' occupied the centre of the cloth, and superimposed on the cross there was a white disc bordered with an embroided silver wreath made from oak leaves and acorns. Inside the white disc there was a black eagle with hanging wings, holding a black swastika.

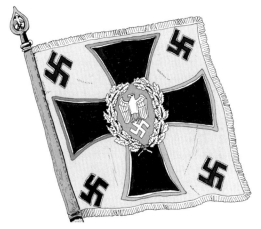

Flag of mountain troops.

During a ceremony the flag was carried by a soldier dressed in regular parade uniform and wearing a gorget – a decorative piece of armour around his neck originally intended to protect the throat. The flag carrier also had a green and white leather bandolier across the shoulder.

The German mountain troops had a number of marching songs. One of their favourites was *Erika*, which is a female name but also means 'heather'. *Erika* (composed by Herms Niel in the 1930s) was also a Waffen SS song. The lyrics of the song have no direct military connection beyond the fact that the narrator (evidently a soldier, though this is not explicitly stated) is away from his faithful beloved and recalls her when seeing the wild plant, which has the same name.

Other popular marching songs were the *Narviklied* (The Narvik Song), *Marsch der Gebirgsjäger* (The Mountain Troops' March), and *Es war ein Edelweiss* (There was an Edelweiss).

Reichskokarde

Another basic insignia was the cockade or rosette, called *Deutsche Reichskokarde*, introduced in March 1933. Worn on headdress, the cockade was circular and made up of the three German national colours: red centre, white or silver in the middle and black outer. On lower ranks' headgear, the rosette was often placed above an inverted chevron with piping. On officers' headgear the rosette was surrounded by a wreath of oakleaves and acorns. As just pointed out, the oakleaf and the acorn combined in a wreath were widely used in Nazi regalia as symbols of strength and an emblematic link with the medieval first German Reich (962–1806).

Reichskokarde (German cockade) with oakleaves.

Arm of service and insignia

Special proficiency arm badges represented a qualification going further than a trade or a speciality. Arm badges (called *Heeres Leistungsabzeichen*) were regarded with more esteem, and distinguished the wearer as possessing special skills and training related to the type of military unit in which he served. This applied for example to prestigious élite formations such as mountain troops (Edelweiss flower), armoured troops (death's

Mountain troopers regarded themselves as members of an elite formation. They were indeed a very special kind of soldier able to operate in the highest peaks, in the worst conditions, in the most inhospitable areas, carrying huge loads of equipment, with little or no shelter, and fighting both enemy and nature. The Edelweiss badge and other insignia contributed to distinguish them and gave them the proud sense of belonging to a special breed. In embroided cloth from the army pattern, Edelweiss was worn on the upper right sleeve. The badge cloth was black; the stamens were yellow; the petals and the edging ropes were white; and the stem and the leaves were green. In a smaller silver-grey metal form the Edelweiss was displayed on the left side of the mountain cap.

head), paratroopers (diving eagle), Africa Corps (swastika on a palm-tree) or Waffen SS (double lightning S rune).

The mountain troops' *Waffenfarbe* (arm of service) was light green, and shown on all headgear piping, shoulder straps and collar patches. The Edelweiss badge – worn on the upper right arm – was machine-woven or machine-embroidered with a green stem, white petals, yellow stamens, and a silver-grey twisted rope-effect border, all on a dark green or grey backing. There was a shining silver-grey metal version of the same design, but without the surround, which was worn on headgear.

The ski Jäger metal badge consisted of a ski overlaid diagonally on a wreath of oakleaves.

Sniper's badge.
Left: First Class; Middle: Second Class; Right: Third Class.

The *Heeresbergführer* badge – worn on the left breast pocket – was a speciality emblem instituted in August 1936 to recognise those Army mountain personnel who were qualified guides.

The Snipers' Badge (*Scharfschützenabzeichen*) was introduced in August 1944. It was awarded in three classes (1st, 2nd, and 3rd), and was worn on the right cuff above all other insignia on the uniform tunic.

Cuff titles

Cuffed titles were a peculiarly German institution called *Armelstreifen*. Adopted by the army before the First World War, they became more significant and widely used during the Second World War. Cuff titles were lettered cloth bands, generally 15 cm wide, for wear around the tunic lower sleeves. They came in many variations and colours (for example dark green, black or brown with silver, white or gold German Sütterlin, Fraktur fount or Gothic lettering). Soldiers in training were usually presented with the cuff title only on completion of instruction, and the award of the title was seen as an initiation rite of passage.

Cuff titles indicated and showed specialisations such as Propagandakompanie (Army reporters and photographers), Feldpost (Army post office units), Feldgendarmerie (military police) or Heeresmusikschule (Army music school) for example. Cuff titles also indicated specific and usually prestigious formations and élite units such as Grossdeutschland (Great Germany Division), Deutsches Afrikakorps (Rommel's North African forces) or Infanterie-Regiment List (the grenadier regiment number 199 in which Hitler had served as corporal during the First World War).

Cuff titles were widely issued to Waffen SS units as distinctive identification (for example 1st SS Division Leibstandarte SS Adolf Hitler, 10th SS Panzerdivision Frundsberg, 17th SS Panzergrenadier Division Goetz von Berlichingen). Cuff titles also commemorated spectacular actions or particular battles (like Spanien, Kurland, Kreta, Afrika) and as such were the equivalent of campaign medals. See below.

Medals

Hitler – as any commander of any army throughout history – cleverly considered that a lot could be done with lavish praise and compliments in the form of medals, awards and decorations flattering human vanity. There were no combat medals specifically created for Gebirgsjäger, but as light infantrymen, mountain soldiers were eligible for all ground troops' medals. Medals were (and still are) the tokens of a nation's esteem. They were awarded in time of war and in time of peace. In time of war medals fell into two main categories.

Individual medals

The first category comprised the world's most famous and coveted medals: the French Légion d'Honneur and the Croix de Guerre, the British Victoria Cross, the United States'

Medal of Honor, and the German Pour le Mérite. Those were awarded for outstanding bravery, for acts of exceptional gallantry and valour to men who had performed in the field. After the defeat of 1918, all existing military orders and decorations for bravery were forbidden in Germany. In September 1939 Hitler reinstated the order of the *Eiserne Kreuz* (EZ, Iron Cross, originally a Prussian decoration) with four grades: Grand Cross (only awarded to Hermann Göring); Knight's Cross (*Ritterkreuz*, about 6,973 awarded); *Ritterkreuz* first class; and *Ritterkreuz* second class. As the war progressed higher grades of the *Ritterkreuz* were added to bridge the gap between Grand Cross and Knight's Cross.

The Knight's Cross with Oak Leaves was introduced in June 1940; Knight's Cross with Oak Leaves and Swords in June 1941 (only 150 awarded) and Knight's Cross with Oak Leaves, Swords and Diamonds in December 1944. The iron cross was fitted to a ribbon round the collar, hung on the left breast pocket or worn on the second button of the tunic (only the ribbon, the cross itself not being shown).

Other new decorations included the German Cross (DK) in two classes and the War Merit Cross (KVK) in five grades.

Specially for brave foreigners fighting alongside with them, the Germans created the Order of Merit of the German Eagle in seven classes.

Other medals and tokens were awarded for military actions: destruction of one or more tanks (*Panzerkampfabzeichen*); shooting down one or more low flying airplanes (for FlaK crews); and participation in infantry combat actions. In order to stimulate the soldiers' interest and skill in marksmanship and to recognize the ability of competent marksmen, a series of lanyards was awarded in varying grades and weapons. The lanyard (aka aiguillette) was a kind of decorated cord hanging between the right shoulder strap and the second button of the tunic.

The *Nahkampfsprange* (close-combat clasp), instituted in November 1942, was awarded for distinguished frontline combat; it was gold for 50 hand-to-hand actions, silver for 30, and bronze for 15. The clasp was worn above the left breast tunic pocket.

The *Infanterie Sturm Abzeichen* (infantry assault badge), introduced in December 1939, was awarded for three successful assault operations on three different

The famous German *Eisernes Kreuz* (Iron Cross) was re-instituted by Hitler in September 1939, and awarded for bravery in combat and distinguished service. It was originally a military decoration in the Kingdom of Prussia, and the German 2nd Reich (1871–1918). Existing in several classes, the cross was derived from the medieval crusader Teutonic Order. It was a pattée cross with four curved arms of the same length, narrow at the centre and broader at the perimeter. It was black with a silver-white outline, and carried the date 1939 and a superimposed swastika in the middle.

Close combat clasp.

days; it was silver for rifle and mountain infantry units, and bronze for motorized formations. It was worn on the left tunic pocket.

The *Verwundeten Abzeichen* (wound badge), re-instituted by Hitler in May 1939 for German volunteers wounded in the Spanish Civil War 1936–1939, was awarded during the Second World War in three classes: gilt for five or more wounds, for total disablement or permanent blindness; silver for three or four wounds, or for the loss of a hand, foot or eye or for deafness; black for one or two wounds. The wound badge, worn on the left breast without a ribbon, was similar to that of the First World War but with a swastika added into the steel helmet.

Verwundeten Abzeichen (wound badge).

This badge, introduced in August 1936, was bestowed regardless of rank. It was both an award and a proficiency mark for men having served as active mountain guides for at least one year. It was a high quality item, oval in shape, with an enamel pin featuring a silver Edelweiss flower bearing the legend *Heeresbergführer* written in black gothic lettering. It was worn on the right breast pocket of the tunic.

Awarded to proficient skiing experts, those badges came as a machine-woven textile patch (left) worn on the tunic's sleeve, and in white/silver metal shape (right) worn on the left side of headgear.

Campaign medals

The second category of medals was for 'just being there', in other words campaign medals. They were awarded without reference to a soldier's personal performance but merely as a recognition of the fact that a man had been involved in a specific campaign, operation, offensive, or battle. Whereas gallantry decorations were usually in the form of a cross, the campaign medals were mostly circular, oval or escutcheon-shaped (in the form of a shield). They illustrated great historical campaigns such as Spain (1936), Africa (1941), Crete (1942), Metz (1944), Kurland (1945) and many others. Campaign rewards also took the form of cuff titles – a cloth band worn on the right under sleeve as previously discussed.

Next to the various official national military decorations, there were also a number of commemorative and individual campaign badges instituted at divisional or regimental level. For mountain troopers these included for example the Narvik medal, the Commemorative Medal for the Caucasus 1942, or the Commemorative Medal for the Polar Front 1942–1943.

This medal instituted in August 1940, was awarded to all personnel having participated to the Narvik campaign in Norway in April 1940. It consisted of a silvered shield on a grey backing cloth. It carried an eagle and swastika insignia, the mention Narvik-1940, and an Edelweiss, a propellor and an anchor indicating the combined participation of mountain troops, aviation and navy.

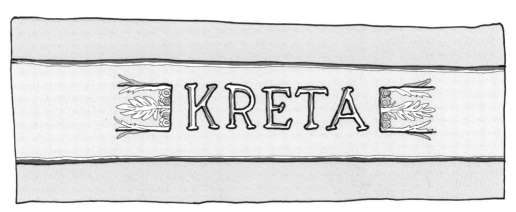

This cuff title, instituted in October 1942, was awarded to paratrooper and mountain personnel of the 5th Mountain Division having taken part in the conquest of the Greek island of Crete in May-June 1941. Worn on the lower left sleeve of the tunic, it consisted of a 3.2 cm broad white cloth strip with golden yellow woven border. In the middle was the legend Kreta in capital letters between two thin branches of acanthus leaves.

The Eastern Medal was awarded to soldiers having served on the Russian Front in Winter 1941–42. Because that harsh period had been particularly cold and had caused many casualties, the medal was sarcastically nicknamed *Gefrierfleischorden* (Order of the Frozen Meat).

The Lapland Shield was the very last decoration issued by the Nazi regime. It was awarded to German military personnel for service in Northern Finland between November 1944 and the end of the Second World War in May 1945. The rather strange medal was crudely manufactured. It consisted of an etched aluminium shield attached to a black piece of cloth. It displayed an eagle (without the usual swastika); mentions 'Lappland' (double 'p' in German); and a map/representation of the Arctic region extending from the Norwegian Sea to the White Sea. The absence of the swastika is explained by the fact that the medal was awarded and produced right after the surrender of Germany in early May 1945, at a time when all Nazi emblems had just been banned. The decoration would have been sewn on the upper left sleeve of the uniform, but it is quite unlikely that they were ever worn. Indeed they were cheap commemorative items from a very recent past awarded and reserved by a few veteran recipients.

CHAPTER FIVE

WEAPONS

Generalities

The seizure of power by the Nazis in January 1933 was the signal for a rapid expansion of German military might. Without serious opposition Hitler swept aside the provisions of the Treaty of Versailles and – from 1935 onward – the German armed forces set into motion long-prepared plans for conscription, the development of a strong Luftwaffe (air force), and Panzerwaffe (armoured force) and for the re-establishment of a military manufacturing industry.

Although German industry gave the lead in new methods of weapon production, she was unable to keep pace with the expansion of her army. The German industry was not prepared for a long war and military programmes had been designed along wrong lines. Nazi Germany took some time to realize that she had started an all-out war, and actually cancelled a number of war contracts after the fall of France in June 1940, because it was thought that the war was over and won. The failure to defeat the USSR and the entry of the USA into the war by the end of 1941 demonstrated that the time of quick victories achieved by Blitzkrieg was over and that the war would last much longer than expected.

It was only in early 1943 that German weapon manufacturing underwent a fundamental change. Economy and industry were totally mobilized and organized for war stemming from the need to make vast quantities of arms in a very short time with the lowest possible cost. After Fritz Todt's mysterious death in February 1942, Albert Speer (1905–1981) replaced him as Minister of Production and Armement. Speer's method was efficient and, between 1943 and 1944, armament production achieved an astonishing success in spite of the intensification of Allied aerial bombardments. Speer's efforts allowed Germany to prolong the war – and the last two years were the most deadly. The huge achievements of the war production, based on private enterprise, improvisation, technical rationality and standardization, were greatly indebted to the technocrat Albert Speer's talented organizational skills. Yet the so-called 'Speer miracle' was not realizable without the ruthless exploitation of human slave labour and the systematic and largescale looting of material resources from occupied Europe.

The Germans also pressed captured weapons into service, but this was not always a blessing as captured weapons were not all excellent, their huge numbers and variety created problems for transport, maintenance, exercise, ammunition, supply and utilization. Furthermore, Hitler constantly acted as if the war was nearly won, he ordered a multitude of rival weapon designs and failed to concentrate on a few good standard types. At the end of the war, when the Germans were forced to a defensive strategy and when they suffered severe fuel shortage under increasing Allied air attacks, Hitler ordered the design and production of huge assault tanks and attack bomber-planes instead of defensive weapons and fighter/interceptor airplanes. Nevertheless, in the light of these difficulties, both in manpower and armament production, it is amazing how the Wehrmacht was able to perform as well as it did during almost six years of war. Despite the shortages of materials, manpower and the Allied air attacks, the quality of German arms was maintained throughout the whole war. Manufacturers showed great ingenuity in standardization and salvaging. Many German designs were further developed in all armies after the war.

A thorough discussion of the history and development of every weapon used in the Second World War by the Germans would need several volumes, for the subject is incredibly vast. The German forces disposed of many service weapons without considering plundered material from the defeated and occupied nations, as well as experimental models, which never saw action. On the whole – in spite of waste and numerous useless (sometimes extravagant) designs – German Second World War weapons were renowned for their quality and flawless performance.

Weapons used by German mountain troops were on the whole the same as the regular German infantry, but naturally greater reliance was placed on lighter weapons than in ordinary combat units. General-purpose machine guns, and an extensive use of mortars tended to replace support artillery. Also in winter and especially in cold weather, additional maintenance, cleaning, and careful handling of weapons, ammunition and equipment was necessary.

Small Arms

Pistol

The Germans did not produce revolvers (aka wheel guns), preferring the advantages of the automatic pistol: larger ammunition capacity than the revolver, quicker reloading (provided a loaded magazine was available), higher muzzle velocity, lightness and

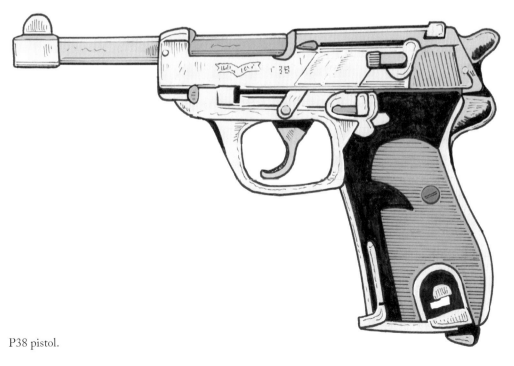

P38 pistol.

compactness. The number of pistols in service in the German Army was enormous. More German soldiers carried pistols than did the Allies, since a pistol in a leather holster was almost a standard part of the equipment even for privates. Pistols – as a symbol of authority – were issued to policemen, senior officers and NCOs but also widely allocated to lower ranks. Pistols were issued on a large scale to infantrymen whose tasks prevented them from using a long-barrelled rifle, such as signallers, drivers, machine gunners, mortar crews, paratroopers, airplane crews, tank and self-propelled gun crews, for example. German pistols included the well-known 9mm Mauser C96, and the quasi legendary Parabellum M 08, which was also called Pistole O8 or P08 or simply Luger after its designer the Austrian Georg J. Luger (1849–1923). Another standard-issue pistol was the modern, safe, cheap and easy to manufacture Walther P 38. This was designed and produced by the Karl Walther Waffenfabriek GmbH from Ulm to replace the Luger. The P38 became the standard Wehrmacht pistol after 1938. It was a remarkable weapon. It had eight rounds in a magazine contained in the grip,

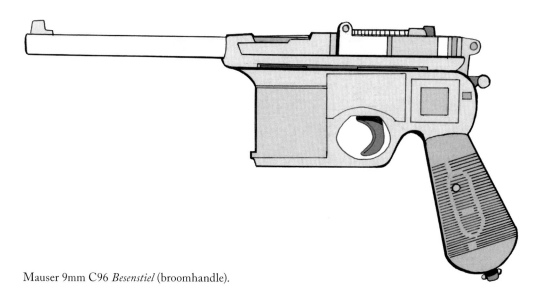

Mauser 9mm C96 *Besenstiel* (broomhandle).

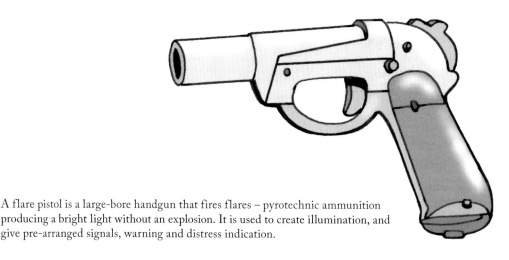

A flare pistol is a large-bore handgun that fires flares – pyrotechnic ammunition producing a bright light without an explosion. It is used to create illumination, and give pre-arranged signals, warning and distress indication.

it weighed 0.96 kg, it was robust, reliable and accurate. The P38 was an immensely successful design widely issued to officers and troops. For signalling in the field several designs were used notably the Leuchtpistole 42 (flare pistol).

Rifle

To accompany their vertiginous scrambling, Gebirgsjäger were issued standard *Maschinenpistole* (submachine-guns), carbines and short rifles. All individual weapons were fitted with a sling for carrying over the shoulder or over the back. The Kar 98 and Gewehr 43 rifles could be equipped with telescopic sights as the distances over which

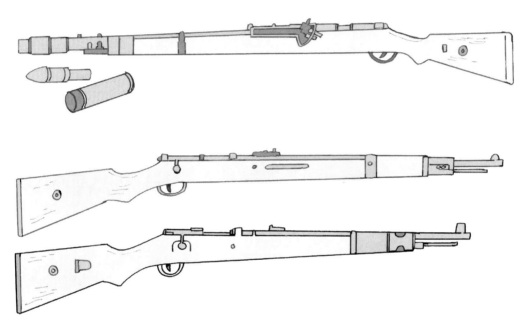

German Second World War rifles.
Top: Gewehr K98K (with grenade launcher); Middle: Gewehr 29/40; Bottom: Mauser G33/40 Carbine.

Rifle Gewehr 24 Mauser.
The rifle came with a number of accessories including strap, cartridge pouches (for five-rounds clip), bayonet with scabbard, and various items for cleaning and maintaining the weapon.

mountain combats took place could be considerable. Accuracy was vital for both small arms and artillery as ammunition was an extremely precious commodity and resupply was not always guaranteed, meaning that every round had to count. When the German infantry was re-shaped and enlarged in 1935, the standard rifle remained the traditional and venerable Infanteriegewehr Modell 1898 and a shortened version of it, the Mauser Karabiner Modell 1898k (Kar 98 K). Special equipment was made for mountain troops including the G33/40 Mauser carbine. Manufactured at Brno in Czechoslovakia, the excellent Mauser G33/40 was essentially a copy of the Czech VZ.33 short rifle. The manually operated carbine weighed 3.7 kg (7.9 lb), it had a barrel length of 19.6 in., it fired the standard 7.92 mm round, and had an internal box-magazine with five rounds.

Sub-machine guns

One of the most formidable Second World War sub-machine guns was the German Erma *Maschinepistole MPi 38*, designed in 1938 and manufactured by the Erfurter Maschinenfabrik Haenel und Suhl, otherwise known as Erma-Werke. The MPi 38 – the most common German sub-machine gun of the war – was very often issued to NCOs or junior officers. A very important and influential weapon, it was robust, short and handy, employing a simple operating system known as blowback to produce automatic fire. It used a low-powered pistol round which was sufficient for short-range accuracy and which made the weapon easy to control. The weapon weighed about 4 kg (8lb 12oz). Its extended length with deployed stock was 832 mm (32.75 in). The Maschinepistole MPi 38 was slightly modified in 1940 (and then known as *Maschinepistole MPi 40*) by the German weapon designer Hugo Schmeisser who made it easier and cheaper to produce. For this reason, both MPi 38 and MPi 40 submachine guns were (and still are) often called *Schmeisser*. But this designation is wrong, because Hugo Schmeisser had – on the whole – only very little to do with the weapons, both being entirely designed by a certain engineer Vollmer for the Erma company. The new Maschinepistole MPi 40 was cruder and less refined than the MPi 38, but – except for small details – it was virtually identical. Its main advantage was the fact that it could be manufactured in separate components and sub-assemblies. Both MPi 38 and MPi 40 had a folding steel stock, simple and strong. They used the same barrel. This was 25 cm (9.8 in) long with six grooves in a right-hand spiral. Both MPi's had a muzzle velocity of about 380 m/s (1,246 ft/s), an effective range of about 100 m (328 ft) and a rate of fire of about 500 rounds per minute. They both used 9 mm Parabellum ammunition, fitted in a 32 rounds detachable magazine.

By the end of the war the Germans developed another automatic weapon known as the *Sturmgewehr 44* (StG-44). This was a gas-operated assault rifle that was about 90 centimetres long and weighed about 5.2 kilograms loaded, with a magazine capacity of 30 rounds and chambered for the 7.92 × 33 mm Kurz (short) cartridge. Combining rifle precision with sub-machine gun high rate of fire, the hybrid and innovative StG-44 is commonly considered to be the first effective assault rifle. The rate of fire of the StG-44 was around 500 rounds per minute and its range was 300 to 600 metres.

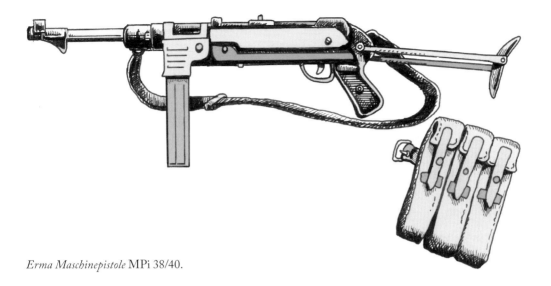

Erma Maschinepistole MPi 38/40.

Erma MPi 38/40 with ammunition pouches clipped on the waistbelt.

Sturmgewehr 44.

Hand Grenades

Extensive use was also made of several types of hand grenades for close quarter fighting. Designed in 1915 and used until 1945, the long-lived *Stielhandgranate* (stick grenade or 'potato masher') is one of the most caracteristic items of weaponry associated with German soldiers. It was a cylindrical charge mounted on a wooden handle. Exploding in a hail of deadly fragments within a range of about 20 metres from the burst, or producing a stunning and lethal blast, the *Stielhandgranate* weighed about 0.59 kg, and was operated by pulling a cord on a friction igniter inside the handle. Another type of grenade used by the German Army was the small and spherical *M 1939 Eiergranate* (egg grenade) which weighed 0.34 kg, could be thrown up to 45 m and had an exploding blast of about 13 m.

Igniting the *Stielhandgranate*.

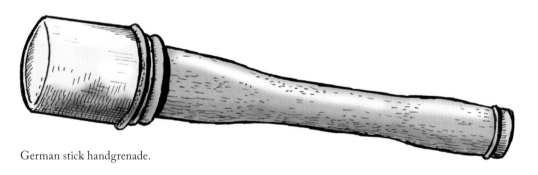

German stick handgrenade.

Machine Guns

During the Second World War the Germans did not produce separate heavy or light MGs but used the dual-purpose air-cooled Maschinengewehr MG 34 and Maschinengewehr MG 42. Air-cooling produced a lighter weapon that one man could carry and operate. Both MG 34 and MG 42 were general purpose weapons combining the characteristics of a light machine gun regarding limited weight, easy manageability, and the formidable fire rate of a heavy machine gun. Both used the standard German 7.92 mm cartridge fed either by a *Gurttrommel* (cylindrical magazine) containing 50 projectiles or by a 250 cartridges belt: the rounds were strung along a belt and joined by metal links, and carried in a metal box. Both German MGs could be adapted on various mountings: as a

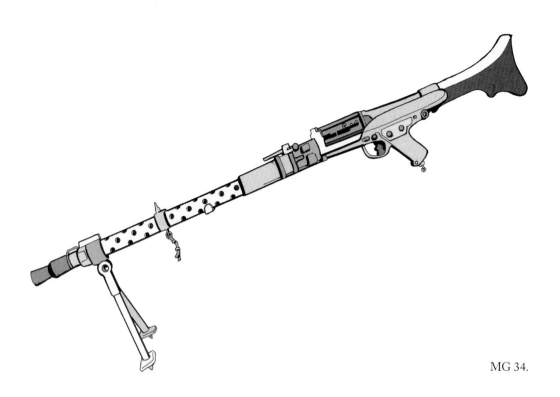

MG 34.

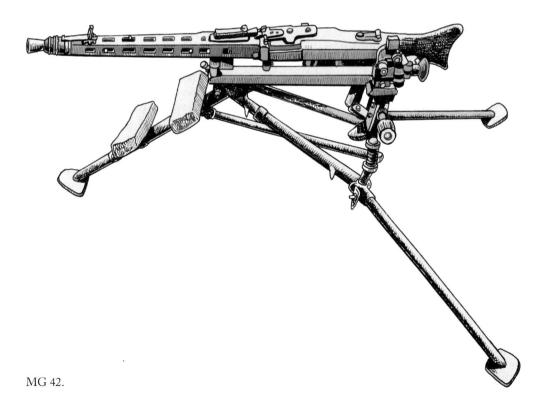

MG 42.

light infantry weapon, they had a folding bipod and shoulder-butt because when firing they were difficult to hold steady. In a defensive role, the MG 34 and MG42 could be fixed on a sophisticated tripod with a long range sight. They could be also used in an anti-aircraft role on a special mount, installed inside a bunker, or placed in a tank or a vehicle as secondary armament.

The MG 34 weighed 12.1 kg (26lb 11oz), it had a length of 1,219 mm (48 in) and could shoot about 800 rounds per minute. The general purpose MG 34 was an excellent automatic weapon but it was complicated to manufacture, it demanded a lot of factory effort to make, it was a costly in materials and time, and rather sensitive to mud, dust and snow. About 200,000 MG 34s were produced in the period 1934–1945.

Designed in 1942, the MG 42 weighed 11,5 kg (25lb 8oz) and could fire automatically up to 1,200 rounds per minute. This high firing rate meant that a large amount of ammunition was required, but the weapon was lighter, faster, cheaper and easier to produce than the earlier MG 34. The MG 42 is often regarded as one of the most effective machine guns produced during the Second World War, being reliable even in the harsh conditions of mountain warfare. An overheating issue that turned the barrel red hot, caused by the formidable rate of fire, was easily solved by immediate replacement, taking only a few seconds and asbestos gloves to protect the gunner from burns. Spare MG barrels were carried in a cylindrical metal case. More than 750,000 MG 42s were manufactured in the period 1942–1945. The MG 42 broke new ground, and is still in use today in many armies throughout the world.

Artillery

Mountain guns

How difficult it was for artillery to be transported and operate in mountainous country cannot be over-emphasized. Mountain warfare obviously required special guns for mobility in difficult terrain. A common feature of mountain guns was that they had a rugged and straightforward design and were rather light. A specific feature of mountain artillery was that it could be quickly dismantled, and transported by pack animals, and easily and rapidly re-assembled for combat. Some mountain guns were deprived of wheels and instead fitted with a skate-shaped undercarriage designed for easy towing over snow by a skiing team, and for flotation so that the gun could be fired off deep snow without digging itself too far in. To match the requirements of mountain troopers, special pieces of artillery were created and manufactured by the Germans. Artillery pieces dating from the Frst World War were used such as the 7.5 cm *Gebirgskannone*, which weighed 613 kg, and the 1918 7.5 cm *leichte Gebirgskannone*, which was slightly lighter. Both guns remained in service until the end of the Second World War.

The 7.5 cm *leichtes Gebirgsinfanteriegeschütz 18* (light mountain infantry gun 18 – in short 7.5 cm leGebIG 18) was originally designed by Rheinmetall-Borsig AG, Düsseldorf, and manufactured by Böhm Waffenfabrik, Strakonitz, Habämfa, located at Ammendorf/Halle. The basic leIG 18 was modified for mountain service in 1935, and production commenced in 1937. The weapon had a calibre of 75 mm, the length of piece (L/11.8) was 885 mm, and weight in action was 440 kg. It fired a shell weighing 5.45 kg to a maximum range (normal charge only) of 3,550 m, with a rate of fire of 8–12 rpm. This gun was intended as temporary equipment until the service début of an improved version designated mountain gun model 36, but remained in service until the end of the war. The 7.5 cm leGebIG 18 could be broken down in 10 loads for pack animal transport. A sled was an optional firing carriage.

Other versions based on this basic design were also used, such as the 7.5 cm *Gebirgskannone 28* and 36 models.

The 7.5 cm *leichte Infanteriegeschütz 18 L/11-8* was issued to infantry, paratroopers, and mountain troops; it broke into six loads of 165 lbs, and was small enough to be carried in a transport airplane Junkers Ju 52.

The 2 cm light FlaK gun 38 had a light variant known as Gerät 239. This dual-purpose anti-tank and anti-aircraft gun featured a modified lightweight tubular tripod version of the 2 cm FlaK 38 mount in order to match the special requirements of mountain units and paratroopers.

The light 2 cm-*Gebirgsflak 38* gun (also called Gerät 239) was issued in 1941 as anti-aircraft and anti-tank gun.

The 7.5 cm infantry/mountain gun IG 18 was issued to German infantry battalions after the First World War for their own close support; this small gun weighed only 400 kg. It was one of the most widely used guns in service with the Wehrmacht. Developed by Rheinmetall in 1927, the gun had a special variant produced in 1939 with small wheels, no shield and the ability to be broken down into four loads – each 140 kg, carried in containers for use by mountain and paratrooper units. It had a range of 3,375 m (3690 yards). Mountain guns were also plundered in the arsenals of occupied countries. The 10 cm *Gebirgshaubitze* (howitzer) was one of the most widely used weapons by both the German Army and the Italian Army. Manufactured by the Czech company Skoda it was not light or easily broken down and thus was not suitable for mountain operations until the development of an adapted version known as 10 cm *Gebirgshaubitze 16* or Gerät 77. This could be broken down easily but only into four large parts which had to be towed by a half-track.

The G36 was a conventional calibre 7.5 cm (3.0 in) howitzer. Introduced in 1938, it was designed by the Rheinmetall Company. It became the standard gun for mountain troops both Heer and Waffen SS. In action the gun weighed 750 kg (1,654 lb), and could be dismantled in eight loads. The weapon fired a 5.75 kg (12.68 lb) shell to a maximum range of 9,250 m (10,120 yards), and had a rate of fire of 6 to 8 rounds per minute. About 1,193 were produced. The versatile G36 was adapted to mountain warfare. The wheels could be removed and replaced with a skate-shaped undercarriage for transport and use in snow.

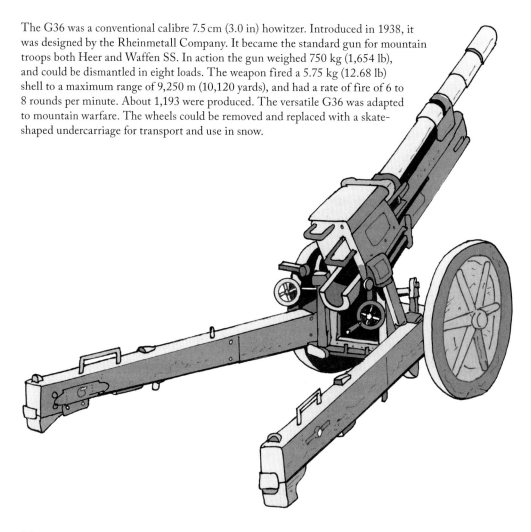

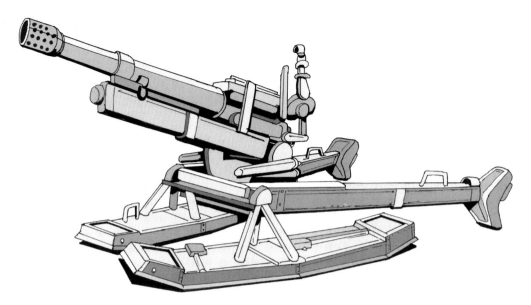

A G36 7.5 cm (0.30 in) calibre howitzer placed on runners for transport on snow.

The Skoda 7.5 cm M15 was designed in 1915 by the Czech Skoda Company, and was used by the Austrian, Hungarian and Czech armies. A number were captured by the Germans in 1938 and used until the early year of the war under the designation 7.5 cm *Gebirgskanone 259*. The weight in action was 613 kg, and maximum range was 8,259 km (9,025 yds).

Captured foreign mountain artillery used by German mountain troops included notably the French 6.5 cm mountain gun that was redesignated *Gebirgskanone 221 (f)*. Other captured French mountain guns featured the redesignated 7.5 cm *Gebirgskanone 238 (f)* and the 10.5 cm *Gebirgshaubitze 322 (f)*. Other captured guns were used, for example Czech guns such as the 10 cm *Gebirghaubitze*, and the Russian 7.62 cm *Gebirgskanone 307 (r)*. The 7.5 cm IG 37 L/22 was a captured Russian barrel mounted on the obsolete German carriage of the 3.7 cm Pak 35/36. The obsolete Norwegian M11 moutain gun designed in 1910 was impressed into German service as the 7.5 cm *Gebirgskanone M11*; the weapon could break into six loads for transport.

Mortars

The mortar is a cheap substitute for the field gun. It is a high trajectory weapon (aka indirect or plunging fire) in which the recoil force is passed to the ground by means of the baseplate. The modern portable infantry mortar (in German *Mörser* or *Granatwerfer* shortened as GrW) was composed of four main detachable parts: a smooth bore barrel, a base plate, a bipod mount, and a sight allowing the user to determine the angle of fire and range. A mortar can be lightweight and gives infantry a mobile close range artillery with a high rate of fire.

The German standard light mortar was the 5 cm *Granatwerfer 36*. This was trigger-fired, operated by a crew of three, and had a maximum range of about 500m. It weighed about 15 kg and broke into two parts (barrel and baseplate) for carrying.

Light 5 cm grenade launcher l.GrW. The trigger-fired light mortar weighed 31 pounds, had a range of 568 yards and broke in two parts for transport.

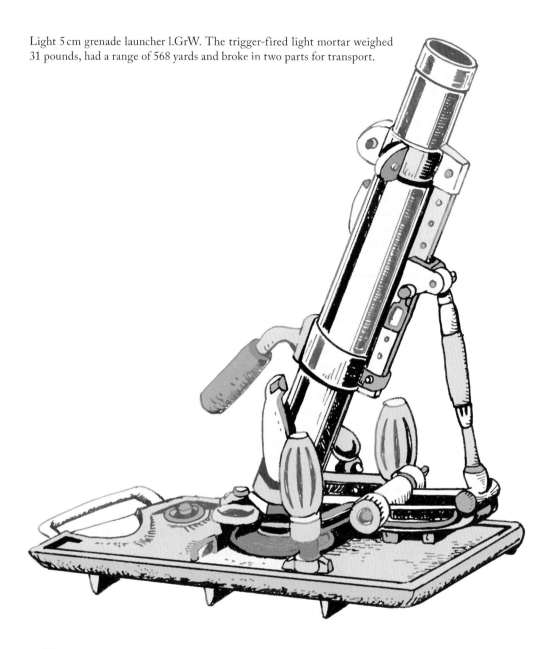

The standard medium infantry mortar was the 8 cm *Granatwerfer GrW 34* which had a maximum range of 1.8 km; the GrW 34 broke in three parts for transportation (barrel, bipod and baseplate). Other German mortars were bomb-launchers such as the heavy *Granatwerfer 42* (ranging up to 6km), and of course many types of mortars captured from the defeated enemy countries. For example Russian mortars such as the 80 cm *Granatwerfer* and the 10.7 cm *Granatwerfer* proved more effective than smaller German models in the snow and were extensively used by Gebirgstruppen.

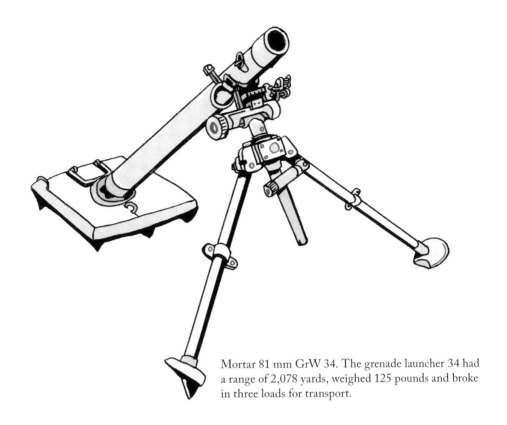

Mortar 81 mm GrW 34. The grenade launcher 34 had a range of 2,078 yards, weighed 125 pounds and broke in three loads for transport.

Portable Infantry Anti-Tank Weapons

Panzerbuchse PzB 39

Based on First World War weapons, the German PzB 39 anti-tank rifle was developed in 1939 at a time when tank armour was still relatively thin. The weapon had a length of 1.60m, an empty weight of 12kg, and fired a high velocity 7.92 × 94 mm armour-piercing cartridge that could penetrate 25mm armour at a range of 300m. After 1942 armour for tanks was thickened to the point that the PzB 39 weapon was no longer effective and was discarded.

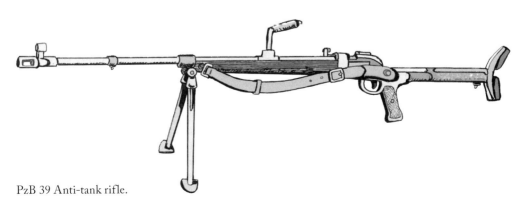

PzB 39 Anti-tank rifle.

Panzerfaust

The Panzerfaust (literally 'armoured fist') introduced by the end of the war was a genuine breakthrough in hollow charge weaponry and anti-tank warfare. It was a one man disposable missile launcher, compact, light and effective at short distances and thus ideal in ambush and defensive warfare in which the Germans found themselves during the last two years of the war. The Panzerfaust was cheap to produce and simple to operate. It entered service in late 1944, it weighed about 5kg (11lbs) and was about 104cm (31 inches) long. It consisted of a disposable steel discharge tube, a blow-off cardboard cap and a percussion igniter fitted near the top and incorporating a basic sight. The warhead was conical in shape, it was stabilized by four spring steel fins, and was held in place by a safety pin which was removed before use. The simple firing instructions were illustrated on the warhead in cartoon form so even non-military personnel (e.g. *Volkssturm* old men, or boys of the Hitler Youth) could use it, as was the case during the last defensive battles in early

The anti-tank Panzerfaust was easy to produce, load, aim, and fire, so it was widely distributed to untrained conscripts in the closing phase of the war.

Firing the Panzerfaust.

1945. There were several variations of the Panzerfaust. The 30M was a small, 10 cm in diameter warhead which could penetrate 150mm of armour at an effective range of 30 metres. There was a variant type 30M which was similar but with a 15 cm warhead. The Panzerfaust 60M and 100M had a modified percussion firing device and propellant charge and were effective at 60 metres and 100 metres respectively. The Panzerfaust's main drawback was its short range which required an audacious, determined and high-spirited operator with nerves of steel. The production of the cheap and successful Panzerfaust peaked at 200,000 units a month in the last year of the war.

Panzerschreck

The German infantry had another close range anti-tank weapon: the 8.8 cm *Panzerbuchse 43 Panzerschreck* (literally 'tank terror' also known as the 'stovepipe'). It was a 5 feet long smooth bore barrel of 8.8 cm calibre firing a 3kg shaped charge projectile powered by rocket propellant. It was actually a direct copy of the American 'bazooka', a specimen of which had been captured in the Western Desert in 1943. Like the US bazooka, the Panzerschrek was a two crew weapon: one man aimed and fired from over the shoulder and an assistant loading the tube from the rear.

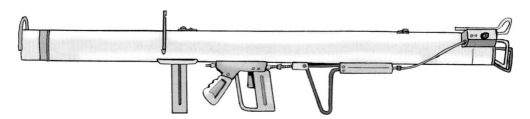

Both Panzerschreck and Panzerfaust had short range, and thus required nerves of steel to use, but the results on enemy armour was devastating in the hands of courageous and accurate marksmen.

Panzerschreck rocket.

CHAPTER SIX

EQUIPMENT

Generalities

Each infantryman carried with him combat, survival and personal equipment to make himself a single unit. The German field accoutrements, based primarily on First World War patterns, were modified and modernized in 1935. By then German combat equipment was standardized though materials and colours varied a lot. The basic *Feldausrüstung* (field equipment) included an integrated system of items designed to complement each other in their wear and practical use. On the whole equipment was relatively lightweight and functional, well-designed, ruggedly constructed, and of a relatively high quality. Of course, the individual field equipment varied according to many factors linked with the rank of the wearer, the kind and length of the mission to be carried out, as well as weather conditions and fighting situations. According to circumstances, and the realities of the battlefield, specialized or specific additional items were brought along and used.

The equipment was issued in various colours, mainly field grey, but many items were matt black, dull dark grey (aka 'Panzer grey'), various shades of dark or reddish brown, olive green and other dark green shades. In winter, items could be painted white or white-washed for snow camouflage.

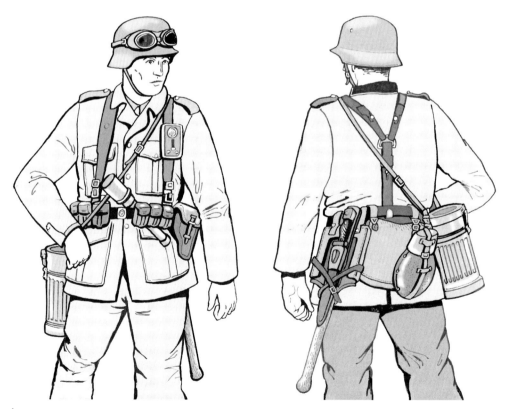

Accoutrements.
Left: Front side with goggles (on the helmet), flash-light, rifle ammunitions pouches and pistol holster.
Right: Backside with entrenching tool and bayonet, breadbag, drinking bottle and gas mask container.

In summer in Europe and in North Africa in the period 1940–1942, in order to withstand the rigours of the hot and dry climate, tropical equipment was issued. This was principally made of canvas and webbing (closely woven fabric) replacing leather, which could stiffen and crack in those conditions. In colour, tropical equipment was mostly light green, light brown, dark yellow, or sand tan.

Just like the uniforms described in Chapter 4, the quality of equipment deteriorated somewhat in the late phase of the war, and in the period 1944–1945 many items were *Ersatz* (substitute) – made of synthetic substances, and materials, cloths, fabrics and components of lower quality from whatever stock was available.

Typically, all uniforms and equipment were ordered to be used until worn out. The Germans were also adept at using captured military stocks and large quantities of Austrian, Czechoslavakian, Polish, Dutch and French items were dyed, recut and tailored in order to match the Wehrmacht demands and style. These makeshift elements were generally issued to German reserve field units, supporting troops, police forces and military auxiliaries.

Basic Equipment

The basic equipment enabled a soldier to survive, operate, and fight effectively in the field for one or two days. This equipment including rations, water, and ammunition weighing about 20lb (ca 9kg). Though specialists were issued a wide variety of items related to their trade, the basic equipment comprised the following.

Waist-belt

Every soldier was issued with a leather service waist-belt. Several models were issued in various materials (leather or web) and colours (brown, black, grey or green). The metal buckle existed in several models too, generally stamped aluminium painted field or matt grey. For NCOs and high ranks, the buckle could be decorated with the national eagle/ swastika within a circular motto reading *Gott mit Uns* (God with us). In service and in the field the belt was used to support various items of standard equipment.

Ammunition pouches

Riflemen's belts were furnished with four or six black pebbled leather cartridge pouches, usually two on each side of the buckle. Each pouch held three loading clips for a total of 45 rounds for the standard 7.92 mm Mauser rifle.

Men armed with MP 38 and MP 40 sub-machine guns were equipped with magazine pouches clipped to the waistbelt. The sub-machine gun pouches (generally three or six) were made from leather or canvas, they were 9in. long and each held six ammunition clips.

Pouches for ammunition magazines for MPi 38 attached to the waist belt.

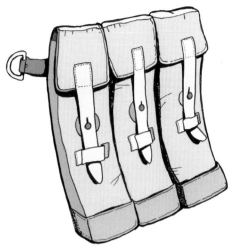

Magazine pouches for the StG44 assault rifle.

Breadbag

Since the early 1800s German soldiers were issued a field grey or olive green canvas bag referred to as *Brotbeutel* (bread bag). It was a simple single-compartment haversack covered with a flap, reinforced with leather or thick cloth at the corners. It was originally intended to carry bread, but its content could include rations, provisions, a small folding field stove, or a metal mess-tin with spoon and fork or various personal items or kits. The breadbag was very often worn over the right rear, it featured buttoned cloth loops enabling it to be fasten to the waistbelt. The breadbag could also feature a special strap allowing it to be slung over the shoulder.

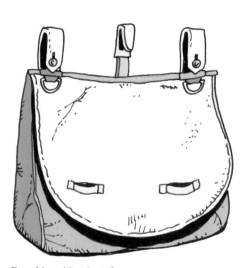

Bread bag (*Brotbeutel*).

Canteen

The German canteen, aka field flask or drinking bottle, came in several variants. It usually contained 0.8 litres (ca 28 ounce), was oval, made of aluminium and in later stages of the war was of enamelled steel, bakelite or plastic. The field flask was covered with a removable, insulating dark green or grey felt cloth which could be humidified to keep the liquid cool for longer. It featured one attached drinking cup made of aluminium. The canteen was attached to the belt usually over the breadbag by means of leather loops.

Cook pot

The cook pot or mess kit, made of aluminum or enamelled steel, was usually carried on the combat pack, although it was sometimes placed into the breadbag or attached to the breadbag in the same way as the canteen, or fastened to the rucksack. Designed for cooking and eating, it had a capacity of 1.7 litres (about 57 ounces), and consisted of two components: a kind of deep pot with a lid, which could be inverted for use as a plate. A combination aluminium fork-spoon was issued to each German soldier. The handles of the fork and spoon were riveted together so that when extended the fork was on one end and the spoon on the other.

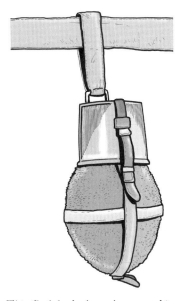

This flask had a loop that passed in the waistbelt which clipped onto the breadbag through a D ring.

Cooking gear (*Kochschirr*).

Entrenching tool

Each man was issued a *Schanszeug* (entrenching tool) for quick digging of field fortification (fox-hole) in case of bombardment – a tedious but life-saving work. It was a short-handled shovel with a square steel blade mounted and riveted to a hardwood 50 cm long handle with a pronounced ball end. The shovel was kept in a black leather cover and hanging from the waist belt on the left side. The entrenching tool existed in several variants, notably as a folding spade copied by the US Army in 1943.

Entrenching tool.

Bayonet

Riflemen were issued several types of bayonet. This was kept in a black leather scabbard with frog, which was often attached to the waist-belt and the entrenching tool, often worn on the left hip.

Pistol holster

Pistols were widely issued not only to officers and NCOs but also to rank and file. The pistol was kept in a leather holster attached to the waist belt. Of course the shape of the holster was adapted to the weapon. Flare pistols were provided a black leather holster, and their rather large ammunitions cartridges were kept in a rectangular box with a capacity of 18 rounds, closed by a lid secured by two straps and studs.

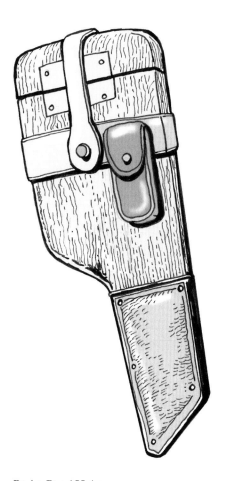
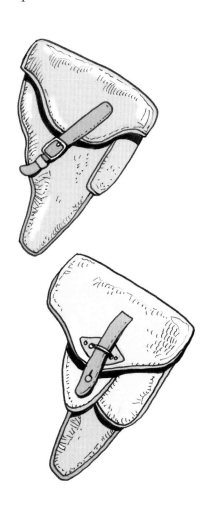

Right: Pistol Holsters.
Holsters for pistols were made of leather and were fixed on the waist belt. Top: Holster for Luger; Bottom: Holster for P38 pistol.
Left: Holster C96.
The holster for the 9mm C96 pistol was a rather heavy and cumbersome item. It was made of wood and could be used as stock for holding against the operator's shoulder for accurate firing.

Machine gun accessories box

Each rifle infantry squad included a portable *Maschinegeweer* (machine gun) – very often a 7.92mm MG34 or MG42. The man carrying and firing that important weapon was issued a distinctive rigid rectangular box covered with a lid. The box was made of hard black leather reinforced with rivets, and featured two loops and a 'D' ring supported by a strap. The gunner's kit box was worn on the waistbelt generally on the right at the front. It contained appropriate accessories, tools and other instruments required to dismantle, clean, maintain and repair the weapon: small replacement spares, an oil container, a cleaning brush, a cartridge extractor, a spare breech, a priming strap, spanners, a small wrench, and firing pins.

The machine gunner (or one of his assistants) was also issued with an anti-aircraft ring sight, a bipod, and a thick asbestos glove or a pad for changing the weapon's barrel, which got very hot after sustained firing for a while. Spare barrels (three or four of them) were housed in a lengthwise-hinged metal protecting case, which was slung behind the back by means of an adjustable web strap. As already discussed in Part 5, the German Second World War MG 34 and MG 42 had a high rate of fire, and were voracious in ammunition, so machine-gun crews had to carry a lot of ammunition (in 50-round belt or 75-round drums) in various steel, aluminium or wooden packing crates.

Map case

Officers and NCOs in leadership positions were issued with articles designed to accomodate their duties. A widely used item was the smooth or pebbled leather report or map case containing a variety of things such as report forms, maps, notebooks, message pads, grid co-odinate scales, a small drafting triangle, writing gear, a whistle or march compass, and service binoculars (held by a strap, and worn around the neck in action). The map case consisted of a flat holder closed by a flap, featuring several ruler and pencil pockets, and two compartments with celluloid map protection covers. The map case was attached by loops to the waist-belt, and generally worn on the left side or front.

Map case for officers and NCOs.

Braces, suspenders, rings and straps

All those items attached to the wearer's waist-belt represented a considerable weight, about 9 kilograms (ca. 20 lbs). In order to help bear and

Belt support.

Belt support (back).

distribute that load, the service waist-belt was assisted by a complementary accoutrement composed of shoulder-belts, a pair of braces or suspenders, rings and straps. The braces were 'Y-shaped' passing from the front of the waistbelt either side of the chest, resting over the shoulders, and converging on a D-shaped steel ring between the shoulder blades. From this ring a single strap joined and hooked to the belt at the centre of the back. The integrated accoutrement was made of black leather or green/greyish canvas. Suspenders and straps were fitted with buckles and studs for individual adjustment. Of course various other items were secured to the suspenders such as a cook pot (mess kit), a small foldaway pocket-size stove burning chemical pellets, additional clothing, weather protection gear (greatcoat or rolled blanket), and food rations and extra ammunition.

The entire individual equipment was well thought-out with a wide variety of carrying positions according to regular prescriptions. Braces and straps evolved to match and suit most of the demands of combat.

Combat pack

Adopted in April 1939, the so-called combat or assault pack was an extension of the Y-shaped braces. The combat pack included an olive green semi-rigid trapezoid-shaped web backpack frame with a small bag as well as hooks, buttons, rings, flaps and straps. Just as the name implies, the pack facilitated the carrying of various items (e.g. weapons cleaning utensils, additional ammunition, rations, cook pot, cloak/tent quarter/poncho, and the like) – in fact everything needed for a short attack, a raid or a limited offensive.

Tarnkappe

An important, popular, and widely used piece of the individual equipment was the *Tarnkappe* (camouflaged cloak). Universally issued throughout the German army, this item was a camouflaged triangular cloak being 203 × 203 × 240 cm in size. It provided an excellent camouflage cloth, and was manufactured from strong tightly woven water-repellent cotton gabardine. In its centre it had a slit with two overlapping flaps, so it could be pulled over the wearer's head and thus worn over the field uniform, and used as an efficient *Regenmantel* (poncho or rain cape) against wind, cold, and rain.

The edges of the cape were furnished with grommets for drawstrings and buttons and holes enabling various combinations providing both excellent protection and freedom of movement for fighting, marching and advancing, as well as horse, bicycle, or motorbike riding. The camouflage of the cloak/poncho was made of various colours and mottle, either the characteristic army camouflage designs or the usual Waffen SS patterns. Some had different make-up on each side, greens predominating on one side and browns on the other. The highly popular *Tarnkappe* was very convenient, as it was multi-purpose. It was also called *Zeltbahn* (quarter tent) as four or more of those triangular cloaks attached together around a small post formed a 9ft high camouflaged pyramid-shaped tent for bivouac.

Each soldier was issued two tent alloy pins and a 2 metre tent-pole section for use when the shelter quarter was made into a tent. The eight-man tent was constructed by

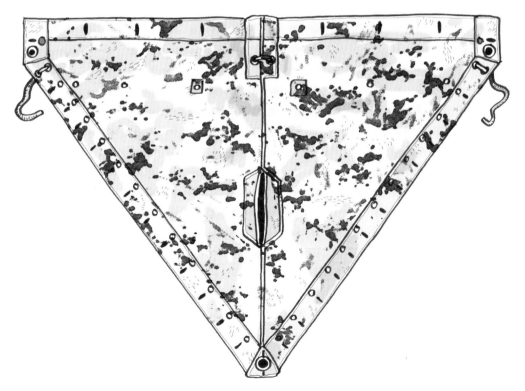

Tarnkappe. The camouflaged cloak aka *Zeltbahn* (tent quarter) combined weather cap, ground cloth, poncho and tent section.

Zeltbahn.
Left: worn as a poncho;
Right: *Zeltbahn* fastened around the legs for marching or riding a motorbike.

pitching two three-sided pyramids and buttoning an inverted shelter half in the space between them. The 16-man tent was made by joining four of the long sides of the eight-man tent. The *Zeltbahn* could be hung overhead to shelter from rain, or provide shadow in hot weather. The loose shelter quarter/poncho could also be used as a stretcher to evacuate a wounded soldier in an emergency, or serve as a shroud for a dead man.

When not used the lightweight *Tarnkappe-Zeltbahn* was tightly rolled and strapped to the bread bag, or attached to the belt support straps on the wearer's back, fastened on the rucksack, or on the combat pack, or on the wearer's field equipment.

Miscellaneous items

In addition there were a number of loose items that could be positioned on each soldier's body. One of these was a wooden handled fighting knife; the knife scabbard was furnished with a spring-loaded hook to fit on to any part of the equipment.

Officers and NCOs were also issued with binoculars with a leather container, eyepiece protector, and a strap allowing the items to hang around the neck. Goggles could be issued and when not worn were carried at the front of headgear – cap or helmet, for example.

Another general issue to all ranks was the *Taschenlampe* (literally 'pocket lamp') – an electrical torch furnished with spring-loaded hook commonly hanging on the tunic breast pocket or to the suspenders. The torch was also a signal device, it could flash and convert white light to blue, red or green.

Grenade pouch

Soldiers who would take part in an assault could be issued with additional stick hand grenades. These were carried in all manner of locations, for example tucked in the boot tops, or tucked in the belt, or in the tunic front. They could also be stored in a sort of musette or knapsack – a simple, strong canvas bag secured by a buckled flap, and featuring a shoulder strap for carrying over the shoulder.

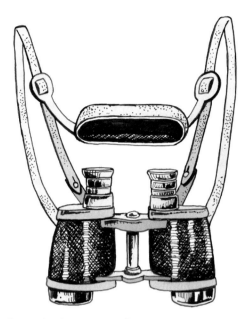

Binocular (*Doppelfernohr*).

Gas mask

The use of terrible toxic gas and other chemical substances during the First World War gave rise to widespread fears of these deadly stuffs during the inter-war period. Therefore German Second World War soldiers on duty always had with them a cylindrical canister containing a gas mask existing in three main models referred to as *Gasmaske* 24, 39, and 38. Made

Most Second World War German gas masks were of the snout type, in which the canister was connected directly to the facepiece. Types GM 30 and GM 38 were in general use, and in addition to the standard masks there were several special types. Generally, German gas masks provided good protection against the common war gases, and fair protection against such gases as arsine, hydrocyanic acid, and cyanogen chloride. The Germans also had three types of gas masks for horses and one for dogs.

of rubberized cloth or canvas or rubber, they included eye pieces, and a filter canister attached to the snout of the face piece. The gas mask was carried in a robust, rather heavy, cylindrical, and fluted canister with a hinged lid, made from corrugated steel. The model M1930 canister was rather cumbersome, being 24.5 cm in length and 12 cm in diameter. The method of carrying for infantrymen prescribed that the cylindrical canister be positioned over the breadbag. It was held by a strap which ran around the right shoulder, and the bottom was hooked to the back of the waist belt. There were several other prescribed less encumbering carrying positions depending on the wearer's duties. For example the gas mask canister could be slung horizontally on the chest and around the neck when riding a motorbike. For mountain troopers it was usually attached horizontally to the back of the rucksack to prevent it interfering with climbing.

As combat poison gas was practically never used in the Second World War, the gas mask was sometimes discarded and the canister converted to a convenient container for various items. A rubberized gas sheet (2 × 1.2 m) was carried in a small rubberized fabric pouch attached to the gas mask canister or attached to the suspenders over the wearer's chest. Each soldier received *Verbandpäckchen* (wound packets) made of grey cloth secured by a string, usually carried inside the tunic's lower right shirt corner.

Backpack

In addition, a backpack or rucksack was issued to carry personal gear, washing kit, rifle cleaning gear, field rations, cooking and eating implements, additional clothing, blankets, tentages and pools, sleeping bags, a length of rope and all other items needed

Tornister (rucksack)
Right: The fur-covered *Tornister* shown here with mess-tin, 'horseshoe' rolled blanket, breadbag and drinking canteen.
Left: Model 1937 Alpine rucksack with 'horseshoe' great-coat, and rolled *Zeltbahn*.

to maintain a group of infantrymen in combat. The *Tornister* was issued in the prewar period and until the beginning of the Second World War it was based on the First World War model, a full marching order, fur-covered backpack generally worn with a 'horse-shoe' rolled blanket, camouflaged shelter quarter, groundsheet and mess tin.

The quaint *Tornister* was progressively replaced by several models based on alpine packs. The German rucksack type 1937 was made of canvas with pockets, flaps and two suspenders. Some heavier models had a wooden frame to provide additional support so that a greater load could be carried. The weight of the full cumbersome kit was important, and in combat the backpack was generally taken off for practical reasons, stored in a truck or left in a dug-out. During action only necessary items were carried on the already discussed combat pack: weapons and ammunition obviously as well as drinking bottle, field dressing, entrenching tool, and gas mask.

Clothing bag

Each soldier was provided with a *Bekleidungssack* (clothing bag), to carry spare clothing items: tunic collar liners, drill uniforms, underwear, socks etc. This was a kind of simple single-compartment satchel-like field grey canvas bag. It was closed by a flap secured by two buckled leather straps.

Individual items

Further individual issues included items that soldiers used for personal hygiene and for the care of maintenance of their uniforms, small arms and others personal necessity equipment. These were obtained from the official military supply companies.

Military forces always stressed the importance of personal hygiene. Healthy soldiers are always efficient, and in any case a fit and clean look was good for morale. All men were vaccinated against various sicknesses.

German military issues were shoe dubbin, brass polishing kits, sewing kits, army soap bars, white cotton towels, tooth powder and brush, utility soap for washing pots and pans. The German discipline required soldiers to be clean shaven, therefore shaving gear and kits were available for troops even at the front. Dispensation not to shave was only allowed under extreme conditions. It was advised to shave at night to avoid chapping of the skin. As a safeguard against lice, the back, the neck, and sides around the ears were cut very short with a little bit of length left on top, often with a parting.

Wisely, a great deal of attention was paid to the infantryman's foot care in the form of foot powder and strict foot cleanliness.

Poor eyesight did not prevent German men from being soldiers and the Army provided spectacles with round wire frame and appropriate circular lenses. The use of sun-glasses and protective goggles was widespread for drivers, motorcyclists, gunners but also for all infantrymen in the open air, particularly mountain troopers.

Every German soldier carried an identification plate, known as 'dog tag'. The German tag was worn around the neck with a cotton cord, it was made of aluminium, and indicated the name, the unit number and the blood type of the bearer; the information was carried on both sides of the two-part tag, so that half the plate could be broken off for dead body identification if needed.

Officers and NCOs were equipped with various items such as watches, binoculars (with leather case and straps usually hanging around the neck), navigation maps (contained in the already discussed leather map-case), marching compass as well as a whistle to give orders by sound. German-foreign phrase books containing phonetic spellings of useful commands and threat were also issued.

Further Army issues included needle and thread to effect running repairs, toilet paper, field dressings, iron rations, vitamins, and stimulant benzedrine tablets (a kind of methamphetamine or 'speed') to keep the men awake longer. Contraceptives were also issued although the military authorities discouraged sexual intercourse with civilian women. Prostitutes allowed to have contacts with Wehrmacht soldiers were carefully checked by the military Health Service. Sex with Jewish and Slav women (considered as *Untermensch*, 'subhuman') was strictly forbidden by the racist Nazi ideology.

As the war progressed and supplies of raw materials dwindled after 1943, the German army was forced to economize on all those items.

Personal gear

Every soldier carried with him personal mementoes which were tolerated but not openly encouraged for security reasons. These items were obtained from religious or charitable organizations, from private purchase, packages from home, booty, or simply picked up along the way. Photographs and letters of family, wives, loved ones, and friends were preciously kept in the wallet. The German Army issued full coloured postcards depicting the Wehrmacht in action as a means of encouraging patriotism. Postcards and letters written by men at the front were strictly censored for strategic reasons, but also for avoiding morale collapse on the Home Front. The keeping of a personal diary and the carrying of watches, expensive jewels and rings were discouraged; occasionally a married man would attach his wedding ring to his identification tag.

Warfare and superstition go together well and the range of small, portable good luck charms, fetishes, amulets and other conjuring talismans was almost unlimited. Though it was strictly forbidden, greed or desire to acquire a souvenir led to stripping the equipment and personal gear of fallen foes, captured prisoners or items stolen from looted civilians.

Personal possessions were generally packed into boxes, clearly marked with the owner's name, rank, unit and regiment numbers. The lucky ones recovered them after the battle. The boxes of the dead were returned to their families.

Mountain Equipment

All previously described equipment was used by mountain troops. In addition the Gebirgsjäger were issued with a number of typical and distinctive items required by the environment in which they operated. As discussed in Chapter 4, mountain troop uniforms included specific combat dress such as heavy duty and warm anoraks, winter suits, and windcheaters which provided some protection against the icy winds and cold weather often experienced in mountains. For fighting, and indeed surviving, in such demanding terrain, special and adequate equipment was supplied. Rock climbing equipment was issued to all Jäger regiments to suit their own personal requirements. Mountaineers were obliged to walk and climb, thus they were equipped with adequate scaling equipment. Many of these climbing items were obviously similar to those used by civilian mountaineers. Basic mountain equipment (carried in rucksack or canvas bags) included the following:

Long, strong, and hard lay ropes and snape links (hooks with a spring allowing the entrance but preventing the escape of a rope); ice-axes (aka pick-axes or piolets fitted with a wooden shaft and an attached leather wrist strap); ice-hammer – a mallet-type head fitted to a short wooden shaft also with a wrist strap; this was used for driving pitons into a rock or crack; pitons were strong heavy spikey pegs featuring a hole at one end through which a rope could be passed to support a climber. For advancing in icy terrain, crampons were used. They consisted of a metal plate or a chain fitted with sharp spikes attached to the soles of the wearer's boots. For marching in deep snow different patterns of snowshoes were issued. They looked like tennis rackets, were flat, roundish or oval and attached to the soles of boots.

Coloured ropes, avalanche markers and flags were used in order to mark out a given route or path. Rope railings were employed for crossing crevasses in glaciers. In poor visibility – such as fog, cloud or darkness – hindrances on the way were fitted with noise making devices such as empty cartridge cases so as to aid orientation. The compass and binoculars were vital pieces of equipment, and were issued right down to squad level. The snow goggles were another essential part of the Gebirgsjäger's kit as they provided protection against harsh winds and were slightly tinted to protect against snowblindness, which might occur at the altitude of 2,000ft and over. Two main sorts were issued: the army goggles were round with plain glass or sometimes a deep brown tint lenses. Very popular and widely used by ground troops were the Luftwaffe goggles designed for air crews. Manufactured by the Leitz company, these had interchangeable curved lenses in plain glass or brown tinted glass for use in bright sunshine or snow. Both goggle types were fixed on a grey leather mask and held by an elasticated and adjustable strap.

Peculiar to the Gebirgsjäger were blankets which did not prove as popular as the captured Russian sleeping bags that equipped Siberian troops and were lighter, warmer and less bulky than the issued German blankets.

Mountain troops were equipped with larger canteens than the regular infantry. The mountain bottle contained one litre (ca 34 ounces) or 1.5 litre. To carry their numerous basic and specialized equipments, mountain troops were issued large rucksacks, which have been discussed above. On the whole typical mountain rucksacks were larger and more versatile than those of the regular infantry. They were olive-drab sack with attached shoulder straps. The item featured a large compartment, some with interior pockets, and closed by a drawstring and a flap. Some had external pockets secured by buckles on the sides. All featured straps, rings and hooks for fastening added equipment. Additional specialized equipment was issued as and when required for specific missions.

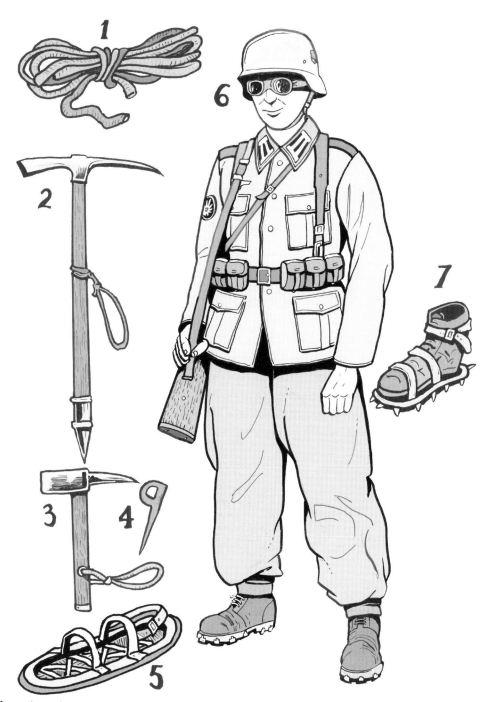

Mountain equipment

1: Rope;

2: Ice pick (piolet);

3: Hammer used to drive pitons into rock;

4: Pitons driven into steep surfaces for rope attachment;

5: Snowshoe made of light wood, cord and leather straps;

6: Goggle and sunglasses were important items because of the glare of blinding light reflected by mountain snow expanses.

7: Crampon attached to the climbing boots for better traction on ice.

Of course skiing-qualified personnel had equipment consisting of skis and ski poles, which were vital for fast movement across snowy winter terrain. German military skis were actually the same as civilian ones. They were made from hard but flexible wood with a white finish, and a green stripe down the centre. All skis, military or civilian alike, are typically pointed and turned up at the front. They featured a fastening Kandahar type footplate to which the skier's boots were firmly attached, which could lead to serious leg injuries.

Small, lightweight, and A-shaped tents were issued to mountain troops, as well as red avalanche cords, avalanche shovels, and avalanche probing poles for rescue work.

As already discussed in Chapter 1, small sleds, known as *akjas* and looking like small 7-foot, flat-bottomed canoes, were used to transport supplies and heavy weapons and evacuate wounded across snow. There were three types: the double-end boat *akja*, the weapons *akja*, and the plywood *akja*. Also, several types of Finnish and Russian sleds were used.

Signal gear

Signals and communications in a mountainous environment have already been discussed in Part 1, so here only a few words are added. As already pointed out communications in high mountainous sites were sometimes difficult and signals soldiers often fullfilled a central role. For the crucial purpose of communication and command wireless radio sets were issued right down to company level but could sometimes be rendered useless by high mountain peaks, which could block radio signals. Compared to today's light,

Portable radio set.

reliable, and modern equipment, German Second World War radio sets were heavy, bulky, fragile, primitive, and necessitated long antennas. They were not always efficient and had to be broken down into mule or man loads for transportation.

For example, early portable radio kits included the *Tornister Funkgerät*. This set weighed 35kg and its transportation demanded a small team, one man actually carried the main apparatus – another the transmitter, another the power batteries and another being the operator. This set had a range of 4km (for voice) or 16km (for Morse signal). Later in the war somewhat lighter radio equipment was developed. The results were devices like the *Feldfunk Sprecher* series or the T-series that could be carried and operated by one or two men. Field telephone with cable was often more reliable than wireless, but more susceptible to damage from enemy action. For establishing field telephone lines, signals personnel were equipped with a cable layer drum fixed upon a kind of portable frame similar to a backpack.

Medical gear

Medical teams operating in mountainous terrain were issued with special stretchers, which allowed the wounded to be lowered vertically down the side of a steep rockface. Medical teams had to deal with several types of injury including wounds caused by firearms and explosions, but also from viral infections caused by cold, snowblindness, frostbite and rope burns, which in some cases could be severe. Medical field equipment included first aid pouches, which were issued to individual combatants. They contained small scissors, suture, haemostat, first aid alcohol pads, ointments and gels, sterile gauzes, swabing compresses, and dressing bandages for treating small wounds in emergency. Everything needed to take care of wounds was carried in adequate bags, rucksacks, and packs by field doctors, assistants and medical orderlies.

In case of severe injury or wounds, when evacuation was necessary, sledges and stretchers on skis were employed for this task. These stretchers could be broken down and had folding legs, which in an emergency could be used as an operating table. Specially designed emergency field tents made of light windproof material, five metres in length were employed to treat the non-transportable wounded. This rather bulky equipment could be broken down into several loads for transport by pack animals. Nevertheless an injuried man in the middle of nowhere in mountainous environment had much less chance of survival than a wounded soldier in 'normal conditions', who could possibly be quickly evacuated, and medically attended without too much delay. Very occasionally (lucky) wounded men could be evacuated by air – provided a STOL (Short Take-Off and Landing) airplane (like the Fieseler Fi 156 Storch), and an airstrip in the vicinity were available.

According to the 1929 revisited Geneva Agreement, medical personnel, their vehicles, tents, and airplanes had to be clearly and conspicuously indicated by a bright red cross placed into a large white disc. This indication also had to be placed on helmets, and on brassards (aka armlets or armbands). Unfortunately, the Nazi regime had little interest in implementing the agreements of the International Red Cross Organization, and the basic principles of the Geneva Convention were often ignored by German forces during the Second World War.

CHAPTER SEVEN

WAFFEN SS MOUNTAIN TROOPS

Sturm Abteilung (SA)

When Hitler started his political career in the early 1920s, his small but aggressive party known as the NSDAP (National Socialist German Workers Party – aka Nazi Party) needed protection during meetings and election campaigns. For this purpose, and also to disrupt other parties' gatherings, provoke disturbance and attract public attention, a private Nazi paramilitary force was created in 1920 called Sturm Abteilung (Assault Battalions) – SA in short, aka Brown Shirts because of the colours of their shirts. Organized by and placed under the leadership of one of Hitler's close political associates, Hauptmann (Captain) Ernst Röhm (1887–1934), the SA militia was one of the instruments, which brought Hitler to power in January 1933.

After the seizure of power, the large, boisterous and radical SA force had actually lost its *raison d'être*, and become a burden to the new Nazi regime, the more so as Röhm had huge political ambitions too. The SA chief saw the SA as the core of the Nazi 'socialist' revolution, and also demanded rewards, sinecures, and positions of responsibility for the leadership of his SA men. Röhm also wanted the SA to be the one and only German armed force, and envisaged replacing the German National Army with his men. This greatly diverged from Hitler's view. Indeed the Führer wanted to gain the trust of the regular army and secure the industrial capitalists' support.

By 1934 there were more Brownshirts than Reichswehr soldiers; by that time, it seems that the SA counted about 2 million members and represented a serious threat for Hitler and the Nazi party. The generals of the regular Heer watched the SA with dislike and considered them as cumbersome rivals. Röhm's radical views alienated the middle classes, the wealthy landowning *Junkers*, the capitalist tycoons, the business magnates, and the top executive industrialists whose support Hitler was so eager to obtain.

In early 1934, the impatient, vociferous and ruthless SA, as well as Röhm's boastfulness, growing greed for power and loose aggressive talk outraged many people, both in and outside the Nazi party. This time the once 'good old pal' had become an insufferable threat to Hitler's power. The SA troops were now a pointless financial burden for the NSDAP, an intolerable challenge to the German army, and an embarrasing force that no longer had any purpose. According to Nazi realities this danger had to be eliminated. Tensions reached

SA Scharfhührer c. 1930.

an explosive point in early 1934. After some hesitations, Hitler acted with chilling decision. In the last weekend of June 1934, Ernst Röhm, and several senior SA officers, as well as several other annoying, opposing and deviating political personalities were savagely murdered in a brutal purge known as the Night of Long Knives.

After the bloody removal, the SA was not abolished, but it never recovered. Until the end of the Nazi regime in 1945, the organization stayed a *Gliederung der NSDAP* (an independent organization within the Nazi Party) but it was reduced in size, and completely deprived of political and military power. Relegated to a backseat role, the SA continued to exist as Nazi propagandists, as street fund collectors, as a veteran and sportive organization and as pre-military training units to the SA Reserve and to the boys of the Hitler Youth.

Schutz-Staffeln (SS)

Together with the SA another Nazi troop was created called the *Schutz-Staffeln* (Protection Detachments, SS in short). Originally the SS constituted a small squad exclusively intended to serve as Hitler's personal close-range bodyguards. Since 1929

Early SS man c. 1925.   SS man c. 1930.

the highly selected SS security guards were placed under the leadership of Heinrich Himmler (1900–1945). Originally the small SS protection group was an administrative part of the SA. When Hitler decided to eradicate the cumbersome and rival Sturm Abteilung and murder their leader Ernst Röhm in June 1934, he entrusted the operation to his loyal SS. As a reward the SS was made a *Gliederung der NSDAP* (an independent part of the Nazi Party) and allowed to develop and grow.

The SS motto was: *Meine Ehre heisst Treue* ('My Honor is Loyalty'), which was displayed notably on the belt buckle. The SS emblem was the typical double Sig rune letters.

From 1934 onward the growth of the SS did not stop. Until the regime's collapse in 1945, the SS was one of the most powerful Nazi organizations in Germany, and in occupied Europe. The SS represented the arrogance of Nazi ideology, and the criminal nature of Hitler's regime. It soon became a central pillar of the Nazi system, a large organization with several main departments, branches and sub-divisions.

SS emblems
Top: Death's Head with crossed bones;
Middle right: Eagle with swastika aka *Hoheitszeichen* existed in both metal and cloth form) with the eagle's wings slightly more pointed than the Wehrmacht's.
Bottom: Double Sig rune. Officially adopted in 1933 by the Schutz-Staffeln of the NSDAP, the Sig rune letter symbolized victory (*Sieg* in German). Designed by SS Sturmhauptführer Walter Heck, the two stricking and fearsome symbolic Sig runes placed side by side like lightning bolts stood for the initials of the SS.

General SS

As just discussed, until June 1934 the SS had been a subordinate branch of the SA. With the bloody purge of the SA in June 1934, the SS had become an independent part of the Nazi Party and needed to be restructured. The *Allgemeine SS* (General SS) was officially created in late 1934 to distinguish its personnel from the military *SS Verfügungstruppe*

The *Sicherheitsdienst der Reichsführer SS* (SD in short) was the intelligence organization and security branch of the SS and NSDAP. In practice members of the SD were part of the Geheime Staatspolizei (State secret police aka Gestapo) created in April 1933 by Hermann Göring. The fearsome Gestapo was a small, secret, and highly effective police service, which carried out the tasks of tracking down and eliminating all dissidents, complainers, and opponents to the Nazi regime. Members of the SD wore the typical SS black or greyish uniform with a black diamond badge bearing the initials SD on the left sleeve, but they could also operate in civilian dress for discreet and sensitive operations. The depicted NCO SD policeman is armed with a Bergmann MP18 sub-machine gun.

SS 1932 black service uniform.

Verfügungstruppe (later known as *Waffen SS*) and the paramilitary *SS-Totenkopfverbände* (concentration camp guards). The Allgemeine SS had full time personnel and also regional units composed of selected volunteering part-time members. It was responsible for administration, management, finance, and enforcing the racial policy and general nazification of Germany. For this purpose the organization included several departments and sub-divisions. Here below only the main SS branches are briefly discussed.

The *Ahnenerbe* was a SS racist society for research and teaching of ancestral 'Aryan heritage'.

The *Lebensborn Verein* was another SS society intended to expand the 'Germanic Aryan race'. The *Rasse-und Siedlungshauptamt* (RuSHA) was the SS Central office for race and settlement, intended to control the 'racial purity' of SS recruits' lineage.

The *Geheime Staatspolizei (Gestapo* in short), and the *Sicherheitsdienst* (SD) were Nazi agencies of security, police, surveillance, and terror. They were tasked with the detection of actual or potential enemies of the Nazi state, the neutralization of any opposition, policing the German people for their commitment to Nazi ideology, and providing domestic and foreign intelligence. In 1936, the *Ordnungpolizei* (Orpo in short) – the regular uniformed security police also comprising the urban and rural police forces, as well as fire fighting brigades – were taken over by the SS. Those instances were purged, Nazified, militarized, and placed under the leadership of SS Oberstgruppenführer Kurt Dalüge. Thereby the official German police was no longer a national force at the service of the population, but another Nazi instrument of control, oppression, and terror. In September 1939, all security and police forces – including the dreaded secret Gestapo and the feared SD – were incorporated into one single centralized large SS police organisation known as the *Reichssicherheitshauptamt* (RSHA or Central Reich Security Office) headed by Himmler's deputy Reinhard Heydrich.

Death's Head Units (SS-TV)

The *SS-Totenkopfverbände* (SS-TV in short, literally 'Death's Head Units') were regiments of wardens and prison guards formed for running the concentration camps (and extermination camps after 1942). The SS-Totenkopfverbände (SS-TV) – originating from Wachtverbände (guard detachments) and Wachmannschaften (guard teams), were composed of permanent professional armed uniformed SS men living in barracks. They had a rudimentary paramilitary training and were originally intended to form *Bereitschaft Truppen* (readiness troops) stationed in key points across the Reich to protect by arms the Nazi regime from any internal revolt. But rapidly – as no such threat appeared – the anti-insurrection force was assigned to run prisons and concentration camps set up by Hermann Göring in 1933 to detain without trial, and 're-educate' all political opponents. The SS-Wachtverbände were indeed closely related with other SS security and repression formations, notably the Gestapo which arrested all opponents to the new regime. Concentration camps and the first regiment of SS-Wachtverbände were organized by Oberführer Theodor Eicke. In 1936 the SS-Wachtverbände were renamed *SS-Totenkopfverbände* (SS-TV 'Death's Head troops') henceforth depending on the SS Hauptamt (SS central office) headed by Obergruppenführer August Heissmeyer.

In time of war the SS-Totenkopfverbände were intended to form a reserve for the Waffen SS (military armed SS), and to the police force, but more than a military formation, the SS-Totenkopfverbände constituted a strictly regulated inflexible repressive machine composed of relentless wardens, jailers, 'screws' and guards of low quality doing the 'necessary dirty work'. Although a branch of the Nazi SS, their expenses were the responsibility of the State.

In early 1940 several Death's Head units were drafted to form a Waffen SS unit called the 3rd SS Panzerdivision Totenkopf. During the Second World War, there were lots of comings and goings between the concentration camp guards, the Allgemeine SS, and the frontline fighting Waffen SS. Many Totenkopfverbände men (at least those physically fit for service) volunteered or were drafted to form *Einsatzgruppen* (literally task forces, in fact a Nazi euphemism for death squads) deployed for mass killing of 'undesirable people' (intelligentia, political opponents and suspects, Jews and Romani) in occupied Eastern territories in Poland and Russia during the war before the creation of the extermination camps.

SS-Totenkopfverbände man 1936.

Members of the SS organizations were also recruited to develop security police units in rear areas, as well as combat brigades and regiments which were transferred to reinforce, provide staff for, or create new Waffen SS divisions, notably the 2nd Das Reich, the 3rd SS Totenkopf, the 6th Nord, the 8th Florian Geyer, the 15th Lettland, the 18th Horst Wessel, the 19th Latvia and the 20th Estland. The duties of guards in the concentration camps were then taken over by senior members of the Allgemeine SS who were too old for active military service, by disabled Waffen SS veterans, by convicts and common criminals, and by pro-Nazi foreign volunteers. During the course of the war, Nazi repression and terror were widely expanded and the number and size of concentration camps grew significantly. The *Inspektion der Konzentrationslager* (Inspection of Concentration Camps) was entrusted to SS Brigadeführer Richard Glucks.

After January 1942, the SS developed in secret the so-called *Vernichtungslager* (extermination camps), which were death camps especially designed for mass murder on an industrial scale by gassing victims and incinerating their bodies in large crematoria. The SS was the organization most responsible for the imprisonment and genocide of about 6 millions Jews, and millions of other victims during the Holocaust (aka Shoah).

Another important SS sub-section was the *SS-Wirtschafts – und Verwaltungshauptamt* (Main Economic and Administrative Office) – a florishing business conglomerate using and exploiting crowds of prisoners, political and racial detainees, slave labourers, and forced workers in work and concentration camps. The management of the concentration camps was placed in 1942 under the authority of the economics and administration main office, headed by SS Brigadeführer Oswald Pohl. By 1943, this SS branch was a huge looting machine that made enormous profits by controlling many activities in the economy, industry, agriculture, construction, armaments projects, and war production, both in Germany and in occupied Europe. The SS economics and administration office had its own workshops and manufacturers, some established inside concentration and work camps where political detainees, prisoners of war, and Jewish inmates were put to work making about 20 per cent of the SS uniforms and equipment. Indeed the SS never went short of forced labour, but increasingly short of raw materials.

Troops at disposal (SS-VT)

Another component of the SS organization were the *SS-Verfügungstruppe* (SS-VT in short, 'troops at disposal') created in 1935. During the First World War, Heinrich Himmler (born in 1900) had been a cadet but was too young to see active combat. The establishment of the Third Reich, the Nazi preparation for war in the period 1933–1939, and the growth of the SS gave him the opportunity to become the heroic military commander he had always wanted to be. In his head Himmler's intention was to create his own SS army – an elite political and military force prepared for war, totally loyal to Hitler, and completely dedicated to the Nazi ideology. The men of the militarized SS-VT units were highly selected (at least before 1943) and harshly trained, fanatically indoctrinated, and ready to obey any of Hitler's order. SS-VT formations were distinct from the police and from the Wehrmacht (German national armed forces). Originally they formed several regiments, which grew to several full divisions at the start of the Second World War.

Waffen SS

Generalities

The designation *SS-Verfügungstruppe* was replaced with the term *Waffen SS* (armed SS), coined by Hitler himself in a speech to the Reichstag in Berlin in July 1940. The SS became a state within the state, and the Waffen SS a private Nazi army within the national Wehrmacht. The Waffen SS became Hitler's own army with its own rules and ethos, and it constituted a serious encroachment into the prerogative of the German regular army. Although Hitler regarded the Wehrmacht as indispensable for his war plans, he suspected the loyalty of much of its leadership, and preferred to place his trust in his own special SS armed forces. Trained to high physical levels, and fanatically indoctrinated in Nazi ideology – Hitler could be sure that the SS and the Waffen SS would eagerly obey and carry out his most extreme plans with devoted blindness, promptitude, and efficiency. The Waffen SS was intended to be a highly selected warrior cast, an 'elite knighthood' forming the spearhead of Nazi Germany's shock troops as Hitler prepared the nation for marching inexorably toward its next war. The Waffen SS indeed became a fight-to-the-death and take-no-prisoners force that was disliked, distrusted, and feared by the regular Wehrmacht.

The Waffen SS was administered by the *Hauptamt Persönliche Stab des Reichsführer-SS* (RFSS – Himmler's personal Headquarter and Staff), and headed by Himmler's assistant Karl Wolf. However, the armed SS forces escaped partly from SS and Himmler's control. The SS authorities did not intervene in the planning, direction and leading of the military operations. This was the exclusive domain of the OKW – *Oberkommando der Wehrmacht* (supreme headquarter of all three German arms) created in 1938, and personally directed by Hitler. It must be pointed out that although the Waffen SS troops were subordinated operationally to the Oberkommando der Wehrmacht, they were never incorporated into the German national Army, but always remained a special subdivision of the SS, which was a *Gliederung* (associated organization), and an integral part of the *Nationalsozialistische Deutsche Arbeiterpartei* – NSDAP in short (German Worker National Socialist Party). Ironically Himmler's Waffen SS succeeded in achieving the very aim for which Ernst Röhm's SA had been crushed in June 1934: the creation of an independent private Nazi armed force.

Regalia

The Waffen SS's organization, units, equipment and weapons were quite similar to the regular army's. However as the Waffen SS was a politico-military organization of the NSDAP, it had its own rank designations, and particular regalia and insignia reflecting its specific status, and distinct political affiliation.

The *Hoheitszeichen* (Nazi official national emblem featuring an eagle holding a swastika in his claws) was worn on the left upper arm of all members' tunics while the regular Wehrmacht soldiers wore it above the tunic's right pocket. In a small silver metal version the *Hoheitszeichen* decorated all cloth headdress. The SS had their own badges of ranks and emblems on the collar patches: the notorious and infamous *Siegrunen*, double SS victory rune commonly described as the 'double lightning flash'. The double SS rune referred to the mythological Nordic past of the 'Aryan' race whose shadowy, hazy, and questionable glories Himmler wished the SS to recreate. The SS runic emblem was shown on vehicles, helmets and flags, documents, administrative forms, and even on typing machines.

Another SS emblem was the *Totenkopf* (Death's Head) with two small crossed bones. In miniaturized metal form, it was worn at the front of most headgear by the SS and by the Waffen SS, and as cloth collar patch by the Panzertruppen (regular army tank troops). The human skull with two crossed femur bones was not a Nazi creation. It was an ancient provocative symbol deliberately expressing defiance of danger and scorn for death, used by pirates of old, and by certain daring nineteenth century military troops.

Units and Ranks

The SS-Verfügungstruppen/Waffen SS were organized and divided into units similar to those of the German ground Army. However, the armed SS was a sub-organization of the NSDAP, and therefore ranks and titles were distinctive to emphasize the total independence and the direct political affiliation of the whole organization. Units and ranks were rather similar to those of the SA, the Allgemeine SS, and all other Nazi paramilitary organizations such as for example the NSKK (Nazi Drivers Corps), the NSFK (Nazi Flyers Corps), the DAF (German Labour Front), and the Hitler Youth. The Waffen SS units and ranks were as follows:

The smallest group was a *Rotte* (squad) counting ten *Schütze* (privates) commanded by a Rottenführer (corporal). Three or four squads formed a *Schar* (platoon) commanded by a Scharführer (sergeant). Three or four platoons composed a *Sturm* (company) commanded by subaltern officers: Untersturmführer (Ustuf, Second Lieutenant), Obersturmführer (Ostuf, First Lieutenant) and Hauptsturmführer (Hstuf, Captain). Three or four companies constituted a *Sturmbann* (battalion) placed under the command of a Sturmbannführer (major or captain). A various number of companies and battalions were regrouped to form a *Standarte* (regiment), aka *Sturmbrigade* (assault brigade) headed by a Standartenführer (colonel). A various number of companies, battalions and regiments formed a division placed under the command of an Oberführer (a kind of general), a Brigadeführer or a Gruppenführer (major general).

Collar patches were made of a small parallelogram (ca. 60 × 40 mm) consisting of a piece of buckram sown to the collar of the tunic, field blouse, and mantle. The right collar displayed the double SS-rune or a divisional emblem, and the left collar indicated the rank of the wearer by means of small silver (or aluminium) embroided square stars, and bars – here that of SS Untersturmführer (Second Lieutenant). For senior officers with the rank of Standartenführer (Colonel) and above, the rank was indicated with oakleaves and square stars placed in both collar patches.

Designation of Waffen SS Divisions

All Waffen SS divisions were designated by a Roman figure and all were given a distinctive name related to Nazism, German history or members' places of origin or nationalities. The Waffen SS divisions were of different kinds according to their speciality.

A *Gebirgsdivision* was a mountain division (indicated by an Edelweiss flower badge worn on the right sleeve).
A *Kavalleriedivision* was a cavalry unit.
A *Grenadierdivision* or a *Waffengrenadierdivision* was an infantry division.
A *Panzerdivision* was an armoured division.
A *Panzergrenadierdivision* was a motorized infantry division.

As racism was a central Nazi tenet, originally members of the Waffen SS were selected on discriminating racial characteristics and strict physical features. However after 1943 selective demands were slackened, but nomenclature and style conferred on the units remained. Indeed designation varied depending on racial composition as follows.

An *SS Division* was composed of 100 per cent *Reichsdeutsche* ('pure' genuine German nationals).

An *SS-Freiwilligendivision* (division of SS volunteers) was formed of *Volksdeutsche* – 'Germanic' northern and central Europeans regarded as 'fellow Aryans' or 'people of similar Germanic blood'.

Finally a *Division der Waffen SS* (division of the Waffen SS) was composed of all non-Aryan 'impure' western, southern and eastern Europeans, both volunteers and conscripted. Those second-class non-Germanic SS men were not worthy of being considered 'Aryan', and were not equal to the 'real genuine and pure' Germanic SS men. For this reason they were not allowed to wear the highly symbolic SS 'double lightning' collar patches. Instead they were issued particular divisional collar patches related to their designation. These discriminating, nonsensical and unnecessary complications were due to Himmler's weird, biased, quasi-religious, obsessed and ridiculous racist credence.

Organization

The senior command of the Waffen SS rapidly realized the advantages offered by mountain formations and six mountain divisions were created. All Waffen SS mountain divisions basically included the same units as the Heer. Each division featured: a headquarters; generally two SS-Gebirgsjäger Regimenter (mountain infantry regiments); one SS-Gebirgsartillerie Regiment (mountain artillery regiment); one SS-Gebirgs-Nachrichtenabteilung (mountain signal battalion); one SS-Panzerjäger Abteilung (anti-tank battalion); one SS-Gebirgs-Aufklarungsabteilung (recce battalion); one SS-FlaK Abteilung (anti-aircraft artillery battalion); one SS-Gebirgs-Pionierabteilung (mountain engineering battalion); and several service companies.

At least that concerned only a few units, as many SS-mountain divisions were under regular strength, particularly those raised in 1944–45. From the start SS mountain divisions (with the exception of the 6th Nord and 7th Prinz Eugen) were intended more for police and anti-partisan warfare than for actual combat role.

On the whole, everything previously discussed about regular mountain troops' training, and weapons may be applied to the Waffen SS mountain divisions, but there were several important differences.

Recruitment

The Waffen SS soldiers were originally composed of highly selected genuine Germans and Volksdeutsche – members of the German speaking community in Europe considered as men of 'similar blood'. The decree of 28 April 1943 marked a decisive turning point for the history of the Waffen SS with bizarre and tragic consequences. Needing still more and more men, not only against the Soviet armies, but against the intensifying guerilla war behind the fronts, Himmler's original stipulations concerning SS racial purity were gradually waived. The acceptance of mercenaries, foreign volunteers, non-Germanic Slavs, and Balkan Muslims into the ranks of the Waffen SS allowed the creation of additional mountain divisions particularly intended for anti-guerilla warfare.

SS Uniforms

Everything discussed earlier about uniforms, combat dress, parade dress, headgear and footwear, weapons, equipment, and special mountain gear can apply to the Waffen SS mountain units. The Waffen SS tended to conform to the Wehrmacht's lead in the design, issue, distribution and allowance of weapons, uniforms and equipment, and complied with the same basic guidelines. However the Waffen SS uniforms, equipment and regalia items were produced in SS factories, manufacturers and workshops employing forced labour in concentration camps ruled by the *SS-Wirtschafts-und Verwaltungshauptamt* (Main Economic and Administrative Office). As already discussed the Waffen SS had their distinctive regalia, emblems and insignia. They also had a wide range of special ammunition pouches in order

Waffen SS steel helmet.

Waffen SS basic uniform.

to accommodate the many models of captured and impounded weapons they used alongside standard issue.

However, and most worthy of notice, the Waffen SS pioneered in developing two important items that formed the universal basis of modern uniforms: the baggy camouflaged smock; and the thick and warm anorak gradually replacing the great coat. Indeed the Waffen SS had more camouflaged field smocks, waterproof anoraks, and windproofs, with matching trousers and camouflaged helmet cover, than regular Wehrmacht troops.

Smock

The typical Waffen SS *Tarnjacke* (camouflage smock) was a collarless, pullover garment made of closely woven spun waterproof rayon/cotton duck. The smock was rather loose and baggy, it was worn over the field uniform, and in cold weather it was sometimes

Waffen SS soldier
wearing camo
smock over *Mantel*.

Waffen SS camouflaged smock (early pattern).
Introduced in 1938, camouflage combat clothing was the Waffen SS's most distinctive trademark. The smock was pullover, worn over the regular uniform tunic. It was produced in several colours (various shades of green, brown, dark yellow and pink), and different patterns referred to as 'plane tree', 'palm tree', 'oakleaf', and 'pea'.

worn over the greatcoat. As a rule no insignia was worn on the smock. It was reversible in order to adapt not only to different types of countrysides but also to seasonal changes. The smock had an irregular 'mottled' pattern of red/brown/pink/grey/yellow tan on one side for autumn wear, and a similar pattern featuring mainly green/brown on the other side for spring and summer wear. A matching cloth camouflage cover was issued for the M35 steel helmet.

As the war progressed a more comfortable version of the smock was issued with a longer skirt, and two proper side pockets with button flaps were added. Buttons replaced the neck drawstring and thin loops and strips of material were sown on the upper arms and shoulders so that fresh-cut leaves, foliage and twigs could be inserted for additional camouflage in the field.

Mantel (overcoat). Issued and worn by all ranks, the overcoat was basically a very long double-breasted garment reaching to the wearer's calf.

Parka

Designed to be worn in cold weather the parka was a windproof, thick, warm, fur- or fleece-lined garment including an integral fur-lined hood. It was rather large, and pulled over the regular uniform. The parka, principally issued to Waffen SS units in 1942, was non-reversible, greyish-green in colour. It had patch breast pockets and slash skirt pockets, and was usually worn without insignia. Later in 1944–45 there was a more convenient variant featuring a fully buttoned front with simple unpleated chest pocket, and this version also came with a variant made up in captured Italian Army camouflage material.

Fur-lined parka.

Feldmütze (forage cap).
The peakless forage cap existed in various styles, designs and quality. The SS *Hoheitszeichen* and the SS Death's Head were shown at the front, and the Edelweiss insignia on the left side of the cap. Note the left collar patch displayed the rank (here that of Untersturmführer), and the right one the SS runes.

Waffen SS *Bergmütze* (mountain cap).
Note the SS metal mountain Edelweiss badge,
worn on the left side of the mountain cap.

SS mountain Edelweiss (textile), worn on the right
upper sleeve of the Waffen SS mountain tunic.

Model 1944 uniform

The pressure of economics in war conditions in the last phase of the war resulted in new uniforms for the Waffen SS. The simplified Model 44 camouflaged combat suit, issued in September 1944 presented some similarities with the British battledress. It comprised a cheap short cammo blouse with only two unpleated chest pockets, and a matching pair of trousers of rather low quality.

Summer uniform

Although the Waffen SS never saw action in northern Africa, the tropical outfit was greatly appreciated in the summer months particularly when campaigning in southern Russia, in the Balkans, Sicily, Greece, and Italy. The tropical uniform – originally designed for the Deutsches Afrikakorps (DAK, German Africa Corps) – was based on the pattern of the regular combat dress, but made from lightweight fabric. It was basically composed of a green-olive or khaki light field tunic often worn open-necked, drill shorts, knee length stockings and canvas topped lace-boots. There were also alternative long trousers in light brown or khaki drill, which were worn full length, and gathered in at the ankle into regular gaiters and studded mountain boots.

Model 1944 uniform.

Summer uniform.

Waffen SS at War

While unspectacular at first, the Waffen SS had a growing impact on Germany's war effort during the Second World War. In all campaigns in which the German forces fought (with the exception of Northern Africa), the Waffen SS made a significant contribution, offering an efficient and professional component that the generals of the regular national Heer simply could not refuse. After the defeat of Stalingrad in January 1943, the surrender of Tunis in North Africa in May 1943, the disastrous battle of Kursk (5 July-23 August 1943), and the successful Allied landings in Normandy (6 June 1944), Nazi Germany was forced to a defensive attitude on three major fronts namely in Italy, in France and in the East. The German armies and the Waffen SS were out-numbered and had to enlist still more unreliable foreigners in their ranks. Although the early divisions were composed of 'pure German Aryans', gradually the corps conscripted and became open to all kinds of foreigners, and most racial selection criteria were relinquished.

What began as an attempt to pool 'Germanic blood' in the Waffen SS ended up as a desperate attempt to recruit anyone in order to stave off the ineluctable downfall. By 1944, Himmler's continued plans for the expansion of his Waffen-SS formation, notably in the Balkans and in Russia, were too optimistic to be taken seriously. Manpower pools were drying up and the willingness of the volunteers dropped with each kilometre the Soviets advanced westward. In most cases the divisions Himmler intended to raise never rose above brigade strength, nor achieved the combat proficiency of the divisions raised and trained in the period 1939–1943. Numbers grew, it is true, but quality enormously dwindled as foreign SS divisions created in 1944–45 fell far below the original demanding standards set for the early divisions. Many of the formations formed in 1944–45 were understrength, badly commanded, and inadequately equipped. As a result their military value was often poor, some were marred with desertions and mutinies, and most were despised by the genuine original German SS.

By late 1944 for a few units, the Waffen SS could no longer be regarded as an 'élite corps'. By 1945, on paper, the Waffen SS formed an army of 38 'divisions', many of which were only improvised brigades, last ditch created regiments, and hastily formed combat groups. However during the last year of the war, a few Waffen SS divisions (notably the twelve first raised) were still determined to fight hard. They were used by Hitler as 'fire brigades' being rushed from one collapsing front to another all across Europe and Russia. Finally the frequency and intensity of the Allied large-scale offensives on all fronts gave the exhausted Waffen SS no chance of rest. They were inexorably driven back, and ultimately they were outnumbered, mauled and defeated. In the end fanaticism proved unable to avoid the final collapse of Hitler's regime.

Although they undoubtely achieved an impressive military record, the Waffen SS troops were neither an ordinary corps nor, as has been often suggested, merely a fourth service of the Wehrmacht. There was indeed a sinister and dark side to the Waffen SS's bravery: a total disregard for human life partly stemming from their belief in themselves as an 'elite' troop who put a low value on others' lives. It must not be forgotten that the Waffen SS were the military standard bearers of National Socialism – a nihilist, violent and destructive ideology that preached Germanic racial superiority and despised 'sub-human' Slavs, Gypsies and Jews.

The controversial Waffen SS built a formidable reputation as a fighting force but they were actually ruthless warriors serving a truly evil cause. It is of course difficult to generalize, and some Waffen SS men were arguably excellent soldiers, but many others were despicable fanatics, ignoble murderers, and abject killers in uniforms. It is biased to infer general principles from specific cases, but it is true, demonstrated and proven that numerous atrocities and war crimes were committed by the Waffen SS, both on and off the battlefield. Besides, the numerous and close connections between the various branches of the SS during the war, make it difficult to consider the Waffen SS as only 'clean, untainted and patriotic soldiers like others'. It was not without reason and not without evidence that the International Military Tribunal held at Nuremberg between

1946 and 1949 condemned the SS (and one of its components, the Waffen SS) as a criminal organization.

The majority of Waffen SS mountain units saw only a few combats against front line enemy forces until the closing phase of the war, and when they eventually did, they suffered high losses. Most Waffen SS mountain divisions were deployed against partisans and guerillas, particularly on the Eastern Front and in the Balkan Peninsula. Most of them were used in police and maintenance of order operations, and their actions usually fell outside the internationally accepted rules of war. Therefore some anti-partisan SS formations behaved with incredible cruelty, and were involved in numerous atrocities and war crimes. Before proceeding with the Waffen SS Mountain divisions, attention must given to guerilla warfare in Nazi occupied countries, and the German response to armed resistance. In order to understand German anti-partisan measures, it is necessary to discuss briefly the characteristics of partisan organizations and their fighting techniques.

Partisans

The combat record of the Waffen SS mountain formations was indeed extremely different to that of the regular German mountain troops. The latter were on the whole 'regular' soldiers fighting against a regular enemy army, the former were mainly security detachments intended to subjugate and suppress partisans and resistants in the occupied areas. The exception was the 6th Waffen SS mountain division 'Nord', which saw significant front line involvement against the Allies.

Mountains – particularly forested ones – made ideal hideouts for elusive guerilla and partisan warfare. Many pockets of resistance remained in northern and central Russia, in Poland, and the Balkan Peninsula in Southeast Europe. Officially the German armies and their allies controlled these territories, but in fact large mountainous, swamp, and forested areas were completely unsafe because of parties of resistance fighters who disrupted German communications and harassed supply lines behind the front. So police and especially trained mountain troops were often employed for anti-guerilla operations.

Partisans (aka resistants) during the war generally consisted of civilians or military personnel and members of defeated armies who took up arms against the German occupiers, everywhere in Europe, particularly in the Soviet Union, Norway, Poland, Yugoslavia, Greece (and Crete), Czechoslovakia, Italy and France. As they lacked proper military backing, training and heavy weapons, these underground groups of highly mobile combatants without uniforms lived off the country, and waged a guerilla warfare with limited attacks, terror and assassination of local collaborators, sabotages, destructions, and skirmishes. Resistance agents and spies would gather intelligence and transmit it to the Allies. Road and railroad bridges were blown; telephone and telegraph lines were cut; trains derailed; German military vehicles, travelling either alone or in convoy, fired on or destroyed and looted; and isolated detachments guarding administrative, economic, industrial and military installations attacked. Small enemy military and police posts were raided to capture weapons. Standing crops were burned, banks robbed, and a general state of uncertainty, demoralisation, disorder and unrest created.

The tactic most commonly practised by partisans was the ambush, so timed that the elusive attackers would be well away before the arrival of any relief. Laying mines and boobytraps, and making demolitions by night were other operations favoured by the guerrillas. Designed to cripple transportation and communications and cause casualties, these tactics created a state of insecurity and nerves, and tied down numerous military personnel who might have been put to other tasks or made available for assignment to active fronts. For example by the end of September 1943, the total strength of German anti-guerilla soldiers deployed in the Balkans was approximately 600,000 – a serious drain on the Third Reich's dwindling manpower resources. After a sudden strike, or when facing strong enemy forces, partisans would swiftly merge with the local populace, or disappear into their hidden bases in remote mountains, swamps and forests.

Armed resistants, maquisards and partisans made significant contributions to the war by frustrating German planning to exploit occupied territories economically. Armed resistance gave significant help to the Allies by providing intelligence, conducting systematic attacks against Germany's rear communication network, disseminating political work among the local population by publishing newspapers and leaflets, and succeeding in creating and maintaining a feeling of insecurity among German occupying forces. To survive, resistance fighters largely relied on the local civilian population. Partisans and maquisards requisitioned food, livestock and clothes from local peasants, and when peasants did not share them willingly, they often took it by force. Local villagers were indeed encouraged or simply coerced into co-operating and supporting the resistance notably by supplying shelter and food, and providing recruits.

Helping the resistance was sometimes involuntary and highly unpopular as partisans would not only requisition food and supplies from the local populace, but also imposed war taxes or contributions to finance their movement. Besides, the activities of the resistance groups always attracted German retaliation and terror on the local populations, notably the arrest and execution at random of hostages among the populations suspected of supporting their enemies. Increasingly and inexorably people were squeezed and pressurized between the German occupiers and the partisans. Often motivated by patriotism, nationalism, political affiliation, but also by ethnic or religious rivalry, personal revenge and hatred, partisans usually took no prisoners, inflicted significant casualties on the occupiers, and greatly disrupted communication and supply lines behind the front. In the last phase of the war, some Resistance groups in Europe and Russia were not only a sideward nuisance for the occupiers. Indeed some had grown in size, and had become more or less genuine, structured, and regular paramilitary formations controlling large zones, and undertaking significant offensive actions in co-operation with the Allied forces.

However resistance movements were sometimes rival and strongly divided by political affiliations, religious and ethnical differences, and occasionally they clashed with one another. In many instances (notably in Poland, Ukraine and in the Balkans for example), the war was a series of internal struggles, local fratricide combats, and regional civil wars within the framework of a major conflict against Nazi Germany and Fascist Italy.

Finally it should be noted that taking arms against the ruthless Nazi occupiers was a risky, courageous and uneasy choice. When captured red-handed, maquisards and partisans were tortured to get intelligence after which they were either shot as terrorists, or deported to a concentration camp. Very often their families, relatives and townsfolk were also victims of merciless retaliation. In spite of their lack of unity, poor co-ordination, and rivalry, partisans caused great frustration to the German occupiers who were not able to fight back with conventional methods.

Armed resistance (and collaboration too) existed in all countries occupied by the Nazis. The subject of this book is Second World War German mountain troops, and not anti-Nazi Resistance in the Second World War. But as German mountain troops (particularly the Waffen SS mountain divisions) were deeply involved in anti-Resistance operations, guerilla and anti-guerilla warfare merits some attention. Not all countries' resistance movements can be discussed here, but the following few concise examples might bring some light on that complex matter.

Polish Resistance

As in many other countries occupied by the Nazis, the situation amongst the Polish partisans was complicated. The largest organization was the nationalist Armia Krajowa, also known as AK (Home Army) formed as early as 1939. There was also a clandestine peasant-armed organization called Bataliony Chlopskie, created primarily for self-defence against the Nazi German abuse. There was also the armed wing of the Polish Socialist Party. There were two Jewish organizations: the Jewish Military Union, whose members co-operated with the Home Army; and the leftist and pro-Soviet Jewish Combat Organization, whose members only took orders from Moscow.

The Gwardia Ludowa (armed groups of the Polish Communist Party) as can be expected, was hostile towards the nationalist Home Army, and collaborated with the Soviet Union. In spite of lack of unity and atrocious German retaliations, the various armed resistance groups were quite active. Amongst many other activities, they launched several important operations including a large sabotage campaign after the Germans started Operation Barbarossa in 1941, and a massive resistance to the German colonisation in the Zamosc district between 1942 and 1944. They staged the Ghetto uprising in 1943, and the Warsaw Uprising in 1944. The Polish resistance mainly fought the Nazis but also against the nationalist Ukrainian UPA, Lithuanian Nazi collaborators, and even the Soviets. It all ended very tragically as most non-Communist Polish resistants were set aside, killed or imprisoned by the 'liberating' Soviets right after the end of the war.

Armed resistance in the Balkans

Occupied for centuries by invading hordes and ambitious empires (Romans, Turks, Austrians, and Hungarians), the people of the Balkan Peninsula (Albanians, Serbs, Bulgars, Turks, Greeks, and other ethnic groupings) have been deeply divided between Eastern and Western cultures, and driven apart by rival, intransigent, intolerant, and irreconcilable religions. This has left the people of the Balkan Peninsula with a legacy of continual hostility, and implacable antagonism regularly bursting out into conflicts and bitter wars. Yugoslavia was a federal country formed by the Kingdom of Serbs, Croats, and Slovenes in the peace settlements at the end of the First World War. It also included Montenegro and the former South Slavic provinces of the Austro-Hungarian Empire, and assumed the name of Yugoslavia in 1929; its capital was Belgrade.

During the Second World War, the mountainous terrain of the Balkan Peninsula, with few good roads or rail lines, hampered the countermeasures of regular forces and made possible sustained guerrilla operations against the German and Italian occupiers. There were actually two main rival partisan factions in Yugoslavia: the Communists led by Josip Broz 'Tito' (supported by the Soviet Union), and the monarchist Chetniks (supported by the western Allies). Chetniks and Communists fought one another and the Germans at the same time. To complicate matters further, there were also guerrilla bands operating under no other authority than their own.

Ukranian Resistance

The Ukrainian Insurgent Army (UPA) was a Ukrainian nationalist paramilitary and later partisan army. Created in 1942 the UPA was involved into a series of guerrilla conflicts during the Second World War against Nazi Germany, the Soviet Union, Czechoslovakia, and both nationalist and communist partisans in Poland. The UPA guerilla groups constituted the armed branch of the political party Organization of Ukrainian Nationalists – Bandera faction (OUN-B) – whose final objective was the re-establishment of a united, independent national state on Ukrainian ethnic territory.

In order to achieve their goals UPA and OUN-B perpetrated ethnic cleansing of the Polish population of Volhynia and East Galicia. They also co-operated with German forces against the Soviets and Poles in late 1943 when the Russians advanced in a western direction. It all ended tragically with the victory of the Soviet Union in 1945, when Ukraine was incorporated into the USSR as one of the Socialist Soviet Republics. In 1991, on the dissolution of the Soviet Union, Ukraine became again an independent republic.

Russian partisans

After Operation Barbarossa in June 1941, remaining units of the mauled Red Army were not captured by the German invaders. Some units decided to keep on fighting. These cores of partisan soldiers were joined by numerous resistants including Jews on the run escaping from the ghettos, teenagers dodging forced work camps, miscellaneous folks and civilians, both male and female, who resolutely chose to continue the combat against the Nazis. Those highly determined opponents joined resistance groups in the forests and urban underground.

In July 1941, the Soviet Central Committee issued instructions for the conduct of 'partisan war' and the Communist Party apparatus, the Komsomol, the NKVD (secret service) and the Red Army were all involved in organizing the movement. The initial results were meagre and scattered, as German counter-measures based on harsh terror and repression curbed many partisan activities, but gradually the long arm of Soviet authority was re-emerging. At the same time the anti-German feeling was growing, and the idea of a 'patriotic war' was intensifying. Soon partisan warfare became a real danger for the Wehrmacht in the German-occupied territories. Official Soviet estimates indicate a total of about 70,000 active partisan combatants in the spring of 1942. By the end of summer, that number had risen to about 125,000.

French maquisards

The term *maquisard* (partisan or resistant) originates from *maquis* – a peculiar scrubland vegetation of the Mediterranean mountainous region, composed primarily of leathery, broad-leaved evergreen shrubs, underbushes, and small trees, where wanted men, criminals on the run, rebels, and guerilla fighters could hide. During the Second World War in France, the term 'maquis' became synonymous with Resistance, and 'maquisard' for Resistant. At first the clandestine French Resistance lacked unity, but in 1943 a National Council was established as the central organ for organizing the armed non-Communist opposition to the Germans, with the support of the British Special Operations Executive (SOE), which was in charge of aiding and co-ordinating subversive anti-Nazi activities in Europe.

After the Nazi attack on the Soviet Union in June 1941, the French Communist Party (which solely obeyed orders from Moscow) entered into resisting the then enemy, and created their own organization. The Communist armed groups were called Francs-Tireurs-Partisans (Free Riflemen-Partisans, FTP), and reluctantly collaborated with the London-based Gaullist resistance and the Western Allies. In summer 1944, all armed resistance groups were merged into the French Forces of the Interior – Forces Françaises de l'Intérieur (FFI). After the Allied landing in France on 6 June 1944, the FFI undertook military operations in support of the invasion, and it participated in the August 1944 uprising that helped liberate Paris. On the whole Resistance groups tried to look like soldiers, but many men wore (outdoor) civilian clothing sometimes with an identifying FFI brassard.

German Responses to Guerilla Warfare

Anti-guerilla fortified posts

The German tendency to underestimate the guerrillas also played its part in their failed struggle against partisans all over occupied Europe and Russia. At first, military commanders felt the suppression of the guerrillas to be a banal function of the police. Later, when things went really bad, and when it became obvious that the police alone could not restore order, the military commanders were forced to have troops taken from the field. However, even after guerrilla activities had turned occupied territories into dangerous theatres of war, Nazi authorities and German military commanders still referred to resistance forces as 'bands' or 'gangs of bandits'.

As a response, the German occupiers patrolled, and guarded sensitive points. The Germans employed armoured trains to protect their rail traffic, and added armed escorts to their convoys on roads. In order to secure vital railroad lines, main road arteries, and all important political, economical and military installations, they established interval fortified posts and strongholds. These strongpoints were actually small forts, heavily armed, and situated in the vicinity of such vulnerable targets as bridges, tunnels, and portions of the rail and road lines difficult to keep under observation from the air or by patrols.

Strongpoints were first occupied by a minimum of one squad, later by a platoon, when the smaller garrisons began to invite attack by the increasingly aggressive enemy. Some forts were of the field type with earthen trenches, and bunkers reinforced and revetted with logs and sandbags; others were elaborately constructed concrete fortifications with accommodation for a permanent garrison. They were situated and arranged in order to deliver all-round fire, and had radio communication with the next higher headquarters and adjacent strongholds. All approaches to the positions were obstructed with obstacles, notably barbed wire, and heavily mined. In addition, mobile and heavily armed reserves – including mountain Army divisions, Waffen SS formations, and locally raised police militias – were kept ready to move immediately to the relief of strongpoints and targets under attack. Partisan activities all over occupied Europe and Russia diverted thousands of German troops from other theatres of war. In addition, they involved extensive use of vehicles, and an expenditure of gasoline the Germans could barely afford.

Search and destroy operations

Large-scale 'search and destroy' operations, and 'pacification and punitive retaliation actions' in the hostile countryside were regularly carried out. Some of those counter-offensives were just small raids, but others were large operations involving many ground troops supported by armour, artillery, aviation as well as paratroopers and gliders dropping troops and materiel. Some operations were successful but many of them were rather useless with unsatisfactory results. Far from being deterrent, large searching expeditions with retaliation, collective punishment, and the careless use of massive firepower in inhabited areas, blind terror and destructions, and 'collateral damage' only increased hatred. Indeed senseless, self-defeating and brutal German occupation policies, mass-murder rampages and vicious anti-partisan actions steadily alienated the population. Nevertheless, in some territories German 'pacification operations' and countermeasures were able to significantly reduce the partisans' activities. Many partisan units went underground, and could not undertake important military operations, but instead were forced to limit themselves to sorting out organizational problems, building up support and establishing a clandestine political influence over the local people. But on the whole the German heavy-handed tactics were ultimately counterproductive. Mopping-up operations sometimes re-established authority but often only temporarily. As soon as troops had withdrawn (they always did, being needed somewhere else) insecurity caused by the partisans' activities started all over again. The partisan guerillas were never eradicated, and more and more large territories escaped German control.

The Germans, of course, did not recognize the legality of partisans. They regarded them as criminal civilians, and called them terrorists or bandits. The partisans' ferocious acts of terrorism incurred savage retaliation by the Germans and their allies, and increased the fury of the struggle. The Germans responded with blind retaliation (like imprisoning and shooting hostages) and counter-terrorism based on collective responsibility. Harsh treatment was therefore handed out to captured partisans and to anyone known or suspected of harbouring or providing assistance to them in any way. Suspects, hostages, captured partisans (and their family members, and local innocent or guilty townspeople) were generally arrested, interrogated, deported to a concentration camp or simply executed without trial shortly after information and intelligence were extracted from them by torture. In some areas, whole populations were deplaced, food confiscated, goods looted, villages burnt, cattle killed or stolen, harvest destroyed in order to isolate partisans and cut them from their supposed support and supply. Atrocities were committed by all sides in a dramatic frenzy and bloody spiral of hysterical violence in which the civil population paid the highest price.

Jagdkommando

A rather efficient German move in anti-guerilla warfare was the creation in the fall of 1943 of the so-called *Jagdkommando*. The *Jagdkommando* (ranger or 'hunting' detachments) were counter-insurgency specialists, highly trained to seek out and destroy guerrilla bands. The idea was based on guerrilla warfare itself, fighting fire with fire, acting and thinking like the enemy, playing their game and beating them at it by setting traps, and ambushes and taking prisoners in order to obtain intelligence. *Jagdkommando* were seldom more than a company in strength, they would hunt, and track down partisans by launching limited counter-raids, and small-scale counter-attacks. These small operations had the advantage of making easier the security of preparations and the achieving of surprise, and keeping partisans constantly on the move.

Personnel of the detachments were usually young and combat-wise (mountain) infantry veterans of German campaigns on other fronts, together with local renegade volunteers. Hardy, physically extremely fit, and thoroughly trained to live in the open for extended periods of time, *Jagdkommando* took over special tasks when situations outgrew the capabilities of conventional military and police units. They were usually lightly armed, depended little on supply columns and could pursue the guerrillas into the most inaccessible areas. When the situation required, the hunting commandos would be quite flexible. In the event they came upon major guerrilla forces, the *Jagdkommando* would rapidly withdraw or keep them under observation and inform battalion or other higher headquarters. While awaiting reinforcements, they would attempt to gather additional information on the guerrilla strength and dispositions.

However, as successful as they were in many small-scale operations, the *Jagdkommando* detachments were never numerous enough to affect decisively the outcome of the anti-guerrilla campaigns.

Traitors

The Nazi occupiers could also try to annihilate local underground resistance networks by infiltrating spies and traitors who were always extremely dangerous. Motivated by hatred, politics, religious or ethnic affiliations, driven by greed, manipulated or blackmailed by the occupiers, these double-crossers were natives who spoke the local language, had extensive knowledge of the towns and countryside, and knew local people and informants. If and when admitted inside a clandestine partisan group or network, those autochthonic renegades would pose as committed members, feign loyalty, but in fact would try to gather intelligence, and when the time was ripe would betray their compatriots. This subterfuge was extremely tricky and difficult to carry out as newcomers, foreigners and strangers were always regarded with suspicion, and submitted to close enquiries before being accepted into a resistance group. Many a resistance network was seized by the Germans owing to infiltrated double-crossers, informers, 'plants' and traitors. Patience, guile, diligence and skill were required, not only for success but for sheer survival. This was a tragic, trickish, subtle, complex, and confusing cat-and-mouse game in which survival or horrible death often depended on sharp instinct, personal cleverness, and psychological talent and skill in detecting in time who was a traitor and who could be trusted.

Foreign auxiliaries

Pro-Nazi governments with puppet regimes were installed in European occupied countries to lighten the administrative and military burden of the occupied areas, and exploit the differences between the various national, religious, ethnical, and political factions. In each occupied country, the Germans encouraged the formation of native police and security forces, and national militias in order to reduce the number of German occupation troops required to keep Nazi order and protect German interests. Those paramilitary and police units guarded sensitive targets, and fought partisans, but they also hunted, arrested, and executed all 'undesirable people' like the Gypsies and the Jews. Here too, not all countries' armed collaboration units can be discussed, but the few following examples might explain this aspect of sensitive collaboration with the Nazis during the Second World War.

In France for example the Vichy regime led by Maréchal Philippe Pétain (1856–1951) allowed the creation of several security organizations, notably the so-called *Groupes Mobiles de Réserve* (GMR, reserve mobile groups) and the hated *Milice Française* (French Militia) especially intended to hunt and fight members of the Resistance. Formed in January 1943 by the Vichy regime (with German aid) the ruthless anti-Resistance Milice Française's formal head was Prime Minister Pierre Laval, but its Chief of Operations and the de facto leader was Secretary General Joseph Darnand. The Milice participated in pro-Nazi propaganda, and in searching for maquisards, and in summary executions and assassinations. They also helped to round up Jews, hostages, and resistants in France for deportation in concentration camps.

In Croatia the Nazis supported Ante Pavelic (1889–1959), the Poglavnik (Prime Minister), who began his collaborationist administration with a ruthless persecution

Members of the French Milice (known as miliciens) wore a large, dark blue, soft Alpino-style beret, a brown shirt, and a dark blue uniform with jacket with matching trousers. During active paramilitary-style operations, a pre-war French Army Adrian helmet could be worn. Their embleem was gamma, the Greek letter G, associated with the Zodiacal Ram, a symbol of virile renewal. The Milice had a small, permanent armed force officially known as the Franc-Garde. Because of the reluctance of the German Army, and the Vichy regime, the Franc-Garde was only slowly and gradually armed. Its officers had pistols from the outset, but it was not until autumn 1943, following the upsurge in attacks against its members, that the Milice and Franc-Garde received some weapons issued by the Germans or intercepted from British airdrops to the Resistance.

Schutzmannschaft in short Schuma (literally Protection teams) were collaborationist police auxiliaries. They were raised on the Eastern Front as early as the winter of 1941 from pro-Nazi local Ukrainian and Russian citizens, as well as Estonian, Latvian, Lithuanian, Belarussians, and Tartars volunteers. They were organized in battalions of about 500 or 700 men led by German officers and NCOs. They wore a typical uniforms consisting of obsolete pre-war Field grey army clothing, and discarded black Allgemeine SS uniforms with original insignia striped, and light blue facing added to cuffs, collars and pocket flaps. Black SS riding boots, and breeches were issued, as well as field hats also with SS regalia removed.

Worn on the upperleft sleeve, the Schuma emblem was a black oval badge surrounded by a wreath of laurel with a swastika, and their motto: Treue, Tapfer, und Gehorsam (faithful, brave and obedient).

of the Serbian minority within the borders of the new Croatian state. Pavelic arrived in Croatia in the wake of the Germans in 1941 with fewer than a hundred of his Ustascha, a fanatical politico-military group. Pavelic quickly organized a pro-Nazi army of fifteen battalions, and a Ustascha Guard of one infantry regiment and a cavalry squadron.

In Serbia the Germans supported General Milan Nedic (1878–1946), a former chief of staff of the Royal Yugoslav Army. Nedic's puppet regime was funded by Nazi Germany, and promoted anti-masonry, anti-Semitism and anti-communism. In March 1942, Nedic established several special police and militarized security forces intended to keep order and lighten the German occupation tasks – notably the Serbian State Guard (Srpska Državna Straža)

The Ustascha was a Croatian fascist, ultranationalist and terrorist organization, which was active between 1929 and 1945. As much of their radical extreme-right ideology was based on Nazi racial theories, members murdered hundreds of thousands of Serbs, Jews, and Roma as well as political dissidents in Yugoslavia during the Second World War.

who together with the SS participated in hunting partisans and Jews, and guarding the Banjica concentration camp at Belgrade.

In Greece, a collaborationist regime (aka Hellenic State) was organized under the premiership of General Georgios Tsolakoglou (1886–1948), who had surrendered the Army of Epirus to the Germans in April 1941. This puppet government's attempts to alleviate the suffering caused by the ruthless German economic exploitation of Greece was completely ineffective, only resulting in a famine that killled about 300,000 Greeks in the winter of 1941–42. The dictatorial Hellenic State also allowed the formation of police and paramilitary units (notably the so-called Security Battalions headed by General Theodoros Pangalos) that actively assisted the German and Italian occupiers in the anti-guerilla war.

The Fiamme Bianche was a unit composed of young men from the Italian Fascist youth movement trained for anti-partisan warfare. The depicted man wears a black beret, a M1941 collarless paratrooper-style jacket over a warm roll-neck sweater, and baggy trousers. He is armed with a FNBA-B M1943 sub-machine gun manufactured by the Fabbrica Nazionale d'Armi di Brescia.

Assessment

The practice of replacing German units with anti-guerilla foreign/local auxiliaries presented several disadvantages – notably limited proper military service, and occasionally duplicity and poor pugnacity, as well as altering and wavering loyalty, and desertion always requiring strict and close supervision by German NCOs and officers. The Nazi and German military authorities were thus always reluctant to arm and develop local, native, non-German militia and anti-guerilla units because of the potential threat they could represent should they rebel, defect, or turn coat. Therefore the Germans generally restricted the strength and number of these paramilitary forces. They employed them for security duties such as the protection of vital roads, railroad lines, and other sensitive targets, and to do the 'dirty work' like blind retaliation operations, arrests, torture, and summary executions.

Once started, the surge of the European anti-Nazi guerrilla movement could not be stopped even by omnipresence of armed guards, large scale military operations and local raids. Infiltration of spies and back-stabbers, arrests and slaughter of innocent hostages, still took place as well as violent retaliation actions, and other atrocities. Just like civil wars, guerilla and anti-partisan warfare were (and still are) extremely brutal forms of armed conflict. Blind terror and equally indiscriminate anti-insurgency warfare, as well as uncontrolled repression, reprisal and retaliation often fuel long-lasting antagonism, and bitterness. They usually generate chaos, irreparable rancour, durable bitterness, ferocious resentment and unforgetable hatred. In the Balkans for example, the bloody conflicts, civil wars, and massacres happening during the break-up of Yugoslavia in the 1990s were directly connected to the tragic Second World War events.

Waffen SS Mountain Divisions

The leadership of the Waffen SS was quick to see the benefits of mountain troops and six mountain divisions were raised, notably the 6th Nord, 7th Prinz Eugen, 13rd Handschar, 21st Skanderbeg, 23th Kama, and 24th Karstjäger divisions. These were especially intended and trained not for conventional warfare in the first place, but as anti-partisan formations notably in the Balkans and in the parts of the Soviet Union they had conquered. This process deliberately exacerbated local antagonism and regional discord, aggravated religious fanatism, worsened racial conflicts, and intensified cultural rivalry resulting in barbaric civil wars.

The military occupation task in the Balkans and in the East was made difficult by the presence of various SS and police agencies in these territories. Acting directly under the Reichsführer SS and Chief of German Police Heinrich Himmler, these police and Waffen SS forces were the cause of constant irritation to the Wehrmacht commanders. Ostensibly responsible for maintenance of order and security, SS activities overlapped those of the military, and local Army commanders were not permitted to control or restrict SS doings, notably the arrests and massacres of opponents and mass murder of Jews and other 'indesirable' people. Waffen SS units on occasion operated without Army control even in the field, and would co-operate in anti-guerrilla operations only when it suited the individual commander and higher SS headquarters.

Various other Nazi agencies, such as the German Foreign Office, maintained some staff intended to accomplish political aims not always consistent with the directives given to the military commanders. In addition, until the defection of Italy in September 1943, Italian military occupying forces were also present in the Balkans, further complicating the task of all Wehrmacht commanders.

6th SS-Gebirgsdivision Nord

The 6th SS-Gebirgsdivision Nord was the first Waffen SS created. Deployed in Finland and Norway in late 1940, for garrison and occupation duties, and in order to watch the borders with the USSR, it was originally formed of conscripted members of the SS Totenkopf (concentration camps 'Death Head' guards). Rather defectively trained and mainly composed of middle-aged inexperienced reservists of SS-TV regiments 6 and 7, the unit fought poorly on the Leningrad front. The rather weak unit was re-organized in January 1942 as Kampfgruppe Nord. In September 1942 it was upgraded to mountain division and improved with the addition of Germans, Finnish, Hungarian, and Romanian volunteers. By mid-1943 when the tide turned against Germany the Finnish contingents were withdrawn from the front. The 6th SS-Gebirgsdivision Nord saw action in Murmansk, Laponia, Carelia and Norway. In 1944 remnants of the unit were divided into several combat groups, which were transferred and engaged on the Western Front, notably in Alsace,

Emblem of the 6th SS-Gebirgsdivision Nord. The unit emblem showed Hagall (aka Hagalaz or Haglaz or Haegl) the ninth rune in the old Scandinavian Viking Proto-Germanic futhark alphabet. Meaning 'hailstone', and corresponding to the letter 'H', it symbolised several things e.g. faith, and intertwined life and death.

Palatinat and Württemberg. Some elements participated in Operation Nordwind during the Ardennes offensive (aka Battle of the Bulge) in winter 1944–1945. Scattered elements of the 6th division Nord were captured by the American forces in Bavaria by the end of the war. Division Nord was the only Waffen SS mountain division to see noteworthy front line combat actions against the Allies. However, it never gained the 'elite' status of other Waffen SS formations like for example the 1st Leibstandarte, the 2nd Das Reich, the 5th Viking, the 9th Hohenstauffen, the 10th Frundsberg, and the 12th Hitler Jugend.

Soldier of the 6th Division Nord. As a German unit, members of the 6th division Nord were allowed to wear the SS runes on the collar patch.

This private of the 6th SS Mountain Division Nord wears the steel Helmet M35 with camouflage cover; the second-pattern pullover smock with foliage loops and skirt pockets; fieldgrey trousers; and gaiters and heavy studded mountain shoes.

Reinhard Heydrich

Men of the 6th Division Nord were not issued a divisional cuffband but in 1942 soldiers of the two main regiments were allowed to wear a cuffband indicating 'Reinhard Heydrich' (SS Regiment 11), and 'Michael Gaissmair' (SS Regiment 12). Reinhard Heydrich (1904–1942) was a high ranking German SS officer, a close collaborator to Reichsführer-SS Heinrich Himmler, and a top police official, and head of the RHSA – the Reich Main Security Office. Heydrich was also one of the main designers of the Final Solution of the Jewish Question (aka Holocaust), and the Acting Reich Protector of Boheme-Moravia in Czechoslovakia. In May 1942 he was ambushed and killed by Czech resistants who had been trained by the British Special Operations Executive (SOE). As for Michael Gaissmair (1490–1532), he was a historical Tyrolean rebel leader during the so-called Deutscher Bauernkrieg (Peasant Wars) in 1524–1525.

7th SS-Freiwillingen Gebirgsdivision Prinz Eugen

The 7th Freiwilligen Gebirgsdivision Prinz Eugen was raised in 1942. Commanded by SS-Gruppenführer Arthur Phlebs (later by SS-Brigadeführer Otto Kumm, and SS-Oberführer August Schmidhuber) it included ethnic-German guards from Banat, and it was the first unit to include in its ranks both ethnic 'racial' Germans, and non-German volunteers (and rounded up men) from Transylvania and Croatia. At first the 7th Division had difficulties getting arms, equipment and supplies, and had to rely upon captured equipment. The 7th Division was composed of two infantry regiments, which were mountain units specially trained to combat Tito's Communist partisans in Yugoslavia, Bosnia and Montenegro where intensive armed resistance virtually paralysed

NCO 7th Freiwilligen Gebirgsdivision Prinz Eugen. After the death of SS General Arthur Phleps (former commander) in November 1944, SS Mountain Regiment 13 was named in his honour, and men were issued a machine-embroided cuffband with the mention Arthur Phleps. The cuffband was made in machine-embroided, flat-wire woven and machine woven forms.

Machine gunner 7th Freiwilligen Gebirgsdivision Prinz Eugen.

German and Italian supply lines. In mid- 1944 the division was engaged for the first time against the Soviet Army in Bulgaria, and as expected suffered heavy casualties. The unit was destroyed while retreating to Croatia, where many men were captured and executed by the Communist Resistance. The historical title of the division referred to Franz Eugen Prince of Savoy-Carignan (1663–1736) who conducted the Austrian army against the French King Louis XIV.

13th Waffen-Gebirgsdivision der SS Handschar (Kroatisch Nr 1)

The 13th Waffen-Gebirgsdivision der SS Handschar (Kroatisch Nr 1), raised in early 1943, was an SS mountain unit composed of Bosnia-Herzegovinan Muslims, both conscript and volunteers. In addition to the conflicts between nationalities within the

Soldier of the 13th Waffen-Gebirgsdivision der SS Handschar. The man wears the regular service uniform including a field grey tunic and matching trousers tucked in puttees. On the left sleeve there is a SS eagle-swastika and a heraldic red/white-chequered schield in the national colours of Croatia, and on the right sleeve the Edelweiss emblem. Headgear is the *Feldgrau* field service felt fez with eagle/swastika and the SS Death's Head at the front. The man is armed with a Maschinenpistole MPi 40.

Fez worn by Muslim men of the 13th Waffen-Gebirgsdivision der SS Handschar. For Muslim Waffen SS troops, Himmler authorized the wearing of the traditional fez – a flat-top conical red peakless hat made of pressed felt. The fez was red for parade and daily service, and field grey for combat. It was of simple construction made of compressed felt, unlined, with a simple sweatband and a black tassel of various length and degree of stiffness. Another fez, conical in shape, and field grey in colour was also worn.

Hauptsturmführer 13th Division Hanschar. The depicted Second Lieutenant wears the conical 'third pattern' fez.

same state and strife between political factions, there was also an important rivalry between religions, mainly between Christian zealots and Muslim fanatics in Yugoslavia. Amazingly, in view of Nazi racist ideology, Hitler and Himmler allowed the formation of Muslim SS troops. This enabled the German occupiers to add fuel to the flames of the Balkan fire by throwing antagonistic religious and ethnic communities against each other. Headed by experienced German Waffen SS officers, the 13th SS mountain unit Handschar was intentionally trained to hunt Tito's Communist partisans in Yugoslavia. Far from the initial SS Germanic 'Aryan' purity, Muslim soldiers wore their traditional fez headdress, made their daily prayers facing Mecca, and had their own imams instead of chaplains. They had the blessing of the pro-Nazi great mufti of Jerusalem, who preached *jihad* – the holy war against unbelievers, Marxists and Jews.

Under the command of SS-Brigadeführer Sauberzweig, the unit was trained in France because the creation of this controversial pro-Nazi formation caused considerable opposition and disquiet in Yugoslavia. At the end of 1943 the 13th Handschar, reinforced with pro-Nazi Croatian Ustachis, was brought back to Yugoslavia. The division hunted partisans in the regions of Bosnia, Zardar and Zagreb, but from the start the unit encountered a lot of issues. The German Nazi leadership tended to treat the Muslim soldiers like *Untermenschen* (subhumans), discipline was bad, hostility grew, mutinies occurred, partisans possibly infiltrated the ranks and fomented troubles, and many men deserted or fought their own war over local issues, looting and murdering Yugoslav Christians.

The Muslim units gained a gruesome reputation for committing numerous exactions against civilian populations. For the German occupiers they proved rather useful in anti-guerilla operations for a while, but when facing determined troops they were a total failure. With the approach of the Soviet forces in late 1944, many more men deserted, while animosity grew to the level of open rebellion. Things went so badly wrong that the Handschar division became unreliable and uncontrollable, so the SS authorities decided to disarm the men and disband it in early 1945. Only the German leadership and cadres kept on fighting in several scattered small combat groups while retreating to Hungary. In May 1945, they surrendered to the British army in Austria. Ethnic and religious confrontations, and ancestral hatred in this region were still the causes of the atrocious unrest and civil wars in the 1990s.

21st Waffen Gebirgsdivision der SS Skanderbeg (Albanische Nr 1)

The creation of the Muslim 21st Waffen Gebirgsdivision der SS Skanderbeg (Albanische Nr 1) was another German attempt to exploit cultural, political and religious rivalry in Yugoslavia. Raised in spring 1944 in Kosovo, it regrouped about 6,500 young Albanian Muslims (of which only 1,500 were retained) with the intention of fighting Albanian communist partisans headed by Enver Hodja. Officially, the 21st was headed by the chief Mostafa Bey Freshery, but actually the real commander was the German SS-Oberführer August Schmidhuber. Due to the low number of volunteers, lack of appropriate equipment and rather low morale, the unit was never fully organized and never reached the intended strength. Against partisans the incomplete SS Skanderbeg 'mountain division' performed rather poorly, but some members were involved in rounding up the Jewish population of Kosovo for deportation, and implicated in atrocities against Serbian civilians in the region. As a military formation Skanderbeg proved largely unreliable, as desertion was very common among the Albanian recruits. The unit was hastily reshaped in late 1944 with German cadres and drafted German members of the Kriegsmarine who fought defensive rearguard actions in their retreat through the Balkans. So the disappointing and short-lived 'division' of Albanian volunteers with a poor record ended the war as a unit composed of German sailors. The designation Skanderbeg was the Germanized version of the name Gjorgy Kaskioka (1405–1468) – a famous 15th century Venitian warlord, adventurer, prince and hero of Albania.

Croatian volunteer in 21st SS mountain division Skanderbeg. The depicted soldier wears the M36 steel helmet. On the left sleeve there was an eagle/swastika, a red badge with the Albanian double-headed black eagle, and a cuffband wearing the mention Skanderbeg. On the right sleeve the Edelweiss emblem was worn. The unit was principally composed of non-German personnel, so members were not permitted to wear the SS collar-patch. Instead they had a distinctive divisional parallelogram cloth collar patch displaying Gjorgy Kaskioka's goat-crested helmet. However this badge was not widely issued so members often wore a plain black patch. The German officers commanding that unit displayed their full SS status by wearing the SS-runes emblem placed on the left breast.

23rd Waffen Gebirgsdivision der SS Kama (Kroatische Nr 2)

The 23rd Waffen Gebirgsdivision der SS Kama (Kroatische Nr 2) was the second unit formed from Croatian Muslims. The designation *Kama* referred to a small dagger used by Balkan shepherds. The unit's cadres were drawn from Reichsdeutsche (Germanic) officers from Hungary and a small number of reliable Muslim men and officers from the disbanded 13th Handschar division.

The Croatian 23rd was created with a similar intention as the Albanese 21st. Raised in June 1944, the unit was placed under command of SS-Standartenführer Helmut Raithel. It should have comprised Waffen SS-Gebirgsjäger Regimenten der SS 55 and 56, each with four infantry battalions, Artillery regiment 24, and the customary support units. However the SS Division Kama was never fully formed. Due to lack of means and under threat of the Soviet advance resulting in low morale and many desertions, the 23rd Kama 'division' (just like the 21st Skanderbeg) was a complete failure. Discipline rapidly deteriorated, many soldiers were sent back home, others deserted, and volunteering remnants of the 23rd were incorporated into several *Kampfgruppen* from the ex-Croatian 13th Handschar. The German cadres were transferred to the 31st Waffen SS Freiwillingen Division Böhmen-Mähren (Bohemia-Moravia) created in March 1944. Both 21st Skanderbeg and 23rd Kama units were officially disbanded in the end of 1944. Then the figure XXIII (23) was given to

Emblem 23rd SS Mountain Division Kama. This Rottenführer (corporal) wears the standard field grey uniform with the Muslim field grey or red fez. A right collar patch showing a 16-point sunflower seems to have been produced but it was never issued to the troops, so members had only a neutral plain collar patch.

the newly formed 23rd Freiwillige Panzergrenadier Division Nederland composed of Dutch volunteers. The despicable divisions Handschar, Skanderbeg, and Kama showed the depth to which Himmler's 'SS elite army' had shamefully descended to fill out the ranks.

24th Waffen Gebirgsdivision der SS Karstjäger

The 24th Waffen Gebirgsdivision der SS Karstjäger was raised in late 1944. The unit originated from an anti-partisan formation known as the SS-Karstwehr Kompanie formed in summer 1942. It was recruited from men who lived in the area known as the Karst, which is situated on the mountainous Istrian Peninsula (today in Northern Croatia). The SS-Karstwehr was intended to fight partisans in the mountains on the borders between Italy, Austria and Yugoslavia. With the Italian surrender in September 1943, the SS-Karstwehr was expanded to battalion strength then to a mountain regiment. It was planned to form a division (that would have been designated the 24th Waffen Gebirgsdivision der SS Karstjäger), but the number of men raised fell way short of those required to constitute a regular division. In 1944, the 24th Karstjäger based in Udine was principally deployed against Communist Italian partisans, and operating between the Istrian Peninsula and the area around Gorizia. By then it had fourteen captured Italian Carro Armato P26/40 medium tanks. In spite of this reinforcement, the unit's strength remained only a brigade composed of a maximum of 3,000 local fascist Italian and 'racial' German, Austrian, Tyrolian, Slovene, Serb and a few Ukrainian volunteers specialised in fighting against partisans. As for the officers, they were drawn from the SS engineer and geological services. In the final phase of the war, suffering the problem of recruitment, casualties and desertion, the 24th Karstjäger was

Soldier of the 24th Karstjäger unit.

still engaged against Communist partisans and also against Allied troops in northern Italy. What was left of the unit merged with remnants of the 7th Waffen SS mountain division Prinz Eugen, and withdrew into the Alps where they continued bitter and hopeless rearguard fighting until the very last day of the war. Survivors retreated to Austria where they surrendered to British forces in May 1945.

Anti-Guerilla Police Units

SS-Polizei Gebirgsjäger Regiment 18

Emblem German police. The typical Gendarmerie-styled orange thread embroided arm eagle and swastika inside a wreath of oakleaves was sewn on the left upper-sleeve.

In 1941, conditions in the Balkans began to make it necessary for police regimental staffs to be set up in order to control a larger area. Regular and permanent police regiments were created, first in Russia then in other eastern occupied territories. A total of 38 Regiments was thus formed.

The SS-Polizei Gebirgsjäger Regiment 18 (SS police mountain regiment) was formed in May 1942 in Garmisch-Partenkirchen (Bavaria) from

Hauptwachtmeister c.1945. During the Second World War, parts of the uniformed Ordnung Polizei (Orpo, order police) were drafted to form anti-guerilla formations, and fighting Waffen SS units – notably the 4th Panzergrenadier Division 'Polizei 1' raised in 1940, and the 35th Grenadier Division 'Polizei 2', raised in early 1945.

three existing Police battalions: Polizei-Bataillonen 302 (Munich), 312 (Innsbruck) and 325. The regiment was at the disposal of the Chief of the Ordnungspolizei (Order Police) SS-Oberstgruppenführer und Generaloberst der Polizei Kurt Dalüge. Shortly after its formation, the unit was sent to northern Slovenia in October 1942 in order to fight against the local partisans. The regiment was headed by SS-Standartenführer (colonel) Hermann Franz who remained in command until August 1943 when he was relieved by Oberstleutenant der Polizei (Lieutenant Colonel) Hösl. All of the police regiments were redesignated as SS police units in February 1943. The SS-Polizei Gebirgsjäger Regiment 18 was sent to Northern Finland by March 1943 and to Greece by October before it retreated north through the Balkans in late 1944–45. While it was stationed in Greece, an artillery battalion was assigned to the regiment. In April-May 1945, what was left of the regiment served as rearguard for General Pannwitz's XV Cossack Cavalry Corps (which consisted mostly of Russians) during the bitter defensive fighting against the advancing Soviet forces. During the three years that it was in existence SS-Polizei Gebirgsjäger Regiment 18 suffered heavy casualties. Of the initial complement of 4,800 men, a total of 3,080 were killed, wounded, captured or missing. The remainder surrendered to the Soviets on the Austro-Yugoslav border at the end of the war.

Lufwaffe Field Divisions

After the heavy casualties of winter of 1941, the German army was in dire need of replacement to bring its infantry formations up to strength. Then the leader of the Luftwaffe, Hermann Göring, reluctantly allowed the creation in September 1942 of air force-controlled field regiments (later divisions, designated Luftwaffe Feld Divisionen LwFD in short) composed of Luftwaffe ground crews and other support personnel. Originally these infantry units were intended for rear echelon security and protection of airfields, bases, supplies dumps, fuel depots, signal stations, and other Luftwaffe structures and installations from guerilla attacks. However,

Oberwachtmeister of the Protection Police Regiment c.1941. The depicted policeman is armed with an Italian 9mm Beretta M38 sub-machine gun. The blowback weapon was large and heavy but it was also robust, reliable, accurate and powerful. It weighed 4.2 kg (9.3 lb) (empty), and was fed by a 10, or 20 to 40 round detachable stick magazine. It had a rate of fire of about 500 rpm, and a maximum effective firing range of 200 m (219 yd). About one million units (in several variants) were produced between 1938 and 1945.

due to Hitler's frantic search for reinforcements, they were immediately deployed in frontline duty principally on the Eastern front. Thrown too quickly into combat, often without a regular complement of support artillery and lacking proper training and leadership, most LwFDs poorly performed. In November 1943 the controversial, unprepared and low-estimated LwFDs were incorporated into the regular Army infantry force. The bulk of the LwFDs remained on the Russian front, but some were used for occupation and anti-guerilla duty notably in Greece, as well as defensive static units in the fortifications of the Atlantic Wall, and in battles in Italy.

CHAPTER EIGHT

CONCLUSION

German Mountain Forces Since 1956

In 1956 the Army of the German Federal Republic (aka West Germany created in 1949) was reactivated. Called the Bundeswehr, it joined NATO during the Cold War, and included a mountain infantry division called the 1st Gebirgsdivision. In 2001 this unit was re-organized and redesignated as Gebirgsjägerbrigade 23. With headquarters located at Bad Reichenhall, the various units of this mountain infantry division were stationed in southern Bavaria in the Northern Alps. Since 2008 the unit has officially been called 'Gebirgsjägerbrigade 23. Bayern (Bavaria)', and according to the official Bundeswehr website, it now totals about 5,300 Gebirgsjäger. The Bundeswehr 23rd Gebirgsjägerbrigade includes the following formations:

- Staff and Signal Company 23.
- 230th Mountain Reconnaissance Battalion equipped with Fennek reconnaissance vehicles and KZO drones;
- 231st Infantry Gebirgsjäger Battalion (Gebirgsjägerbataillon 231), deployed at Bad Reichenhall equipped with GTK Boxer armoured personnel carriers, counting about 900 infantrymen divided into five companies;
- 232nd Gebirgsjäger Battalion (Gebirgsjägerbataillon 232), counting about 900 soldiers divided into five companies, stationed at Bischofswiesen;
- 8th Mountain Engineer Battalion (Gebirgspionierbataillon 8) based at Ingolstad; 8th Mountain Supply Battalion based at Füssen; 230th Mountain Pack Animal;
- Operations and Training Centre operating at Bad Reichenhall.

The mountain division 23 is part of the so-called Stabilisierungskräfte (stabilisation forces). Every infantry battalion includes one Schwere Jägerkompanie (company) armed with heavy mortars, anti-tank weapons and 20 mm guns.

Today, the modern German Gebirgsjäger still share a number of traditions, notably very close comradeship and distinct *esprit de corps*. They wear the regular Bundeswehr grey uniform with the characteristic Bergmütze (mountain cap). The traditional uniform (Berganzug) is still rooted upon the alpine mountain climbing dress. It includes a Skibluse (lightweight grey ski tunic); Keilhose (thick and warm black trousers), which during the summertime are replaced with Kniebundhose (knee-breeches quite similar to knickerbockers); and Bergstiefel (heavy, ankle-height mountain boots). Of course all Nazi insignia and emblems of the past have been proscribed since 1945. However, the traditional *Leontopodium Alpinum* (Edelweiss flower) has been re-introduced as a distinctive emblem and is still worn on the left side of the cap, stem to the front.

BIBLIOGRAPHY

Augusta, Pavel, *Encyclopédie de l'Art Militaire*, Paris: Ars Mundi Editions, 1991.

Bartov, O., *L'Armée d'Hitler, la Wehrmacht, les Nazis et la Guerre*, Paris: Hachette Littératures, 1999

Bender, R. and Taylor, H.P., *Uniforms, Organization and History of the Waffen-SS*, Bender Publishing, 4 Volumes, 1969–75.

Blockmans, Willem, *Oorlog door de Eeuwen heen*, Hilversum: HD Uitgeverij, 1977.

Bowood, Richard, *Soldiers*. London: Paul Hamlyn Ltd, 1965.

Buchner, Alex, *Die Deutsche Gebirgstruppen: Der Kampf der deutschen Gebirgsjäger an allen Fronten 1939–1945*. Podzun Pallas Verlag.

Carman W.Y., *A Dictionary of Military Uniform*. London: Book Club Associates, 1977

Cecil R., *Hitler's War Machine*, London: Salamander Books Ltd. 1976.

Chamberlain, Peter, and Gander, Terry, *Infantry, Mountain, and Airborne Guns.* London: McDonald and Jane's, 1975.

Chant Christopher, *The Nazi War Machine*, London: Tiger Books International 1996.

Clancey, Patrick and Jewell, Larry, Transcription of: *Technical Manual Handbook on German Military Forces* (TM-E30–451). The Pentagon, Arlington, Virginia: US War Department, 1945.

Cooper, L., *Swastika at War.* London 1975.

Corvisier, André, *Dictionnaire d'Art et Histoire Militaires*, Paris: Presses Universitaires de France, 1988.

Crefeld, Martin van, *The Art of War*, London: Smithsonian Books-Cassell, 2002.

Deighton, L., *Blitzkrieg.* Triad Ltd Granada, 1979.

Delagarde, J., *German Soldiers of World War Two*, Paris: Histoire & Collections, 2005.

Ehrlich, C., *Uniformen und Soldaten –Ein Bilndericht vom Ehrenkleid unserer Wehrmacht*, Berlin: Verlag Erich Klinkhammer 1942.

Fitzgibbon, Constantine, *A Concise History of Germany*. New York: The Viking Press, 1973.

Fochler-Hauke, Gustav, *Schi-Jäger am Feind*. Kurt Vowinckel Verlag, Heidelberg 1943.

Fritz, Stephen, *Frontsoldaten: The German Soldier in World War II*. University Press of Kentucky, 1997.

Funcken, L. and F., *L'Uniforme et les Armes des Soldats de la Guerre 1939–1945*, Paris: Editions Casterman 1972.

Gander, T., *Military Archaeology* Cambridge 1976.

Gordon-Douglas, S.R., *German Combat Uniforms 1939–1945*, Edgware: Almark Publications, 1970

Gunter, Georg, *Die deutschen Skijäger bis 1945*. Podzun-Pallas, Friedberg 1993.

Halder, J.U., *Das Taschenbuch für den Winterkrieg, Anhang 2 zur H.Div.1a (Handboek on Winter Warfare).* Oberkommando des Heeres: August 1942

Hubatsch, W., *Hitlers Weisungen für die Kriegsführung* Frankfurt am Main 1962.

Kaltenegger, Roland. *Deutsche Gebirgsjäger im Zweiten Krieg*. Motorbuch Verlag 1998

Keegan, John, *Encyclopedia of WW2*. Feltham: Bison Books/Hamlyn Publishing Group Ltd, 1977.

Keegan, John, *A History of Warfare*. London: Hutchinson 1993.

Landemer, Henri, *Les Waffen SS*. Paris: Balland, Livre de Poche, 1972.

Lefèvre, Eric, *Uniformes de la Wehrmacht*. Paris: Argout- Editions, 1979.

Lepage, Jean-Denis, *An Illustrated Dictionary of the Third Reich*. Jefferson N.C. McFarland & Co, Inc., 2014.

Martin, Paul, *European Military Uniforms*. London: Spring books,1963

McInnes, Colin and Sheffield, G.D., *Warfare in the Twentieth Century, Theory and Practice,* London: Unwin Hyman 1988.

Mitcham, Samuel W. Jr., *German Order of Battle. Volume Two: 291st – 999th Infantry Divisions, Named Infantry Divisions, and Special Divisions in WWII.* PA; United States of America: Stackpole Books, 2007.

Mollo, A., *German Uniforms of World War II*, London: MacDonald & Jane's, 1976.

Montgomery, Bernard, *A Concise History of Warfare*, Ware: Wordsworth Editions Ltd. 2000.

Munoz, Antonio, *Obscure Combat Formations of the Waffen SS*. Axis Europa Books 1991.

Oswald, W., *Kraftfahrzeuge und Panzer der Reichswehr, Wehrmacht und Bundeswehr.* Motorbuch Verlag Stuttgard 1971.

Schellens, J.J., and Mayer, J., *Histoire Vécue de la Seconde Guerre Mondiale.* Verviers: Editions Gérard & Co (Marabout Université), 1962.

Tagg, M., *De Wereld in Oorlog.* Harmelen: Ars Scribendi BV, 1993.

Taylor, H.P., *Germanische SS, 1940–45*, Historical Research Unit/Uniforms of the SS series, 1969.

Tessin, Georg, *Die Landstreitkräfte 1—5. Die Verbände und Truppen der deutschen Wehrmacht und Waffen SS im Zweiten Weltkrieg 1939—1945.* Frankfurt am Main: E.S. Mittler, 1965.

Wright, Quincy, *A Study of War*, Chicago: Phoenix Editions, 1965.

Young, Peter, *The Fighting Man*. London: Orbis Publishing, 1981.

Zoeft, Wolf T., *Seven Days in January*. Bedford PA: Aberjona Press, 2001.

INDEX